Whispers of His Power

Daily Devotional Readings

Whispers of His Power

Daily Devotional Readings

Amy Carmichael

A DOHNAVUR BOOK

But these are only hints of His power, only
the whispers that we have heard.
Who can know how truly
great God is?

Job 26: 14 (Good News Bible)

PUBLICATIONS

Fort Washington, PA 19034

Whispers of His Power

Published by CLC Publications

U.S.A.
P.O. Box 1449, Fort Washington, PA 19034

GREAT BRITAIN
51 The Dean, Alresford, Hants., SO24 9BJ

ISBN (mass market): 978-1-61958-041-1
ISBN (e-book): 978-1-61958-053-4

Copyright © 1982
The Dohnavur Fellowship

First published in England 1982
by SPCK/Triangle Books
First American edition 1993
by Christian Literature Crusade
Fort Washington, PA

This printing 2012

Introduction

Amy Carmichael was a British missionary who arrived in India in 1895 and stayed there till her death in 1951. At first she worked in the villages of South India. Then in 1901 she began to make a home for children in need of protection and care. Others came to help her, and the Dohnavur Fellowship was born, named after the village in Tamil Nadu in which it is situated. For fifty years she was Mother to an ever-increasing family and saw many of her children grow up to serve the Lord by serving others.

An accident in 1931 led to illness which confined her almost entirely to her room for the remaining years of her life. During that time she continued to counsel and encourage all who came to see her and wrote many books and innumerable letters.

She also wrote notes to her "family" almost daily, in which she shared the thoughts the Lord had given her. They were intended only for her "children," but a selection has already been published as daily meditations, called *Edges of His Ways,* and the following notes are from some of the remaining material. She wrote to her family:

It is a great cheer to know that these notes are sometimes a help. There are so many of you, and your needs are so various and your ages so different, that it is impossible any one word should be for everybody. No archer ever shot several hundred targets with one arrow. But if any arrow finds its target I am content — and grateful.

I don't want you to be spoon-fed children, but to get your food direct from your Heavenly Father. But this is my only way to reach you, my own dear children, and I often read things I long to share with you, and sometimes our Lord Jesus speaks a word to my heart which I think would speak to yours.

It has been necessary to edit the notes and remove many purely topical allusions. A few written to young children have been included, together with many to older members of her family and especially to those taking part in the many branches of the work — caring for children, teaching, helping the sick in our hospital, and doing routine work such as cooking and sewing and housework.

The work at Dohnavur and its various outposts continues today, and in addition many hundreds of Old Boys and Old Girls are scattered throughout India and in other countries. As you read these notes, will you pray that Amy's children may continue to follow the teaching and example she gave

6

them, and live to serve and glorify the Lord and make His love known to others.

B.M.G. TREHANE
Dohnavur Fellowship

NOTE ON BIBLE TRANSLATIONS

Unless otherwise stated, biblical quotations are from the King James Version of the Bible.

The following abbreviations are used to refer to other versions and sources:

BCP	Book of Common Prayer, the Great Bible of Coverdale
Conybeare	W. J. Conybeare, *The Epistles of Paul* (a translation)
Delitzsch	F. Delitzsch, *Notes on Job and the Psalms*
Kay	W. Kay, *The Psalms* (a translation)
Septuagint	The Septuagint
Moffatt	J. Moffatt, *The New Testament: new translation*
Rotherham	J. B. Rotherham, *The Emphasized Bible*
RV	Revised Version (1881)
Way	A. Way, *The Letters of St. Paul* (a translation)
Westcott	B. F. Westcott, *Notes on the Gospel of St. John*
Weymouth	R. F. Weymouth, *The New Testament in Modern Speech*
Young	R. Young, *A Literal Translation of the Bible*

Verses of poetry without quotation marks were written by Amy Carmichael.

January 1

Who then is a faithful and wise servant whom his
Lord hath made ruler over his household,
to give them meat in due season?
Matt. 24:45

This morning as I read of the faithful and wise servant, who gave food in due season to his Lord's household, I felt he had at least the great help of being with his fellow-servants. He could not help knowing what kind of food to give to one and another, and also he would know the proper season. Whereas I can't be with you, and so I can't watch as I would wish to do, and have the right sort of food ready for the particular season.

At last I found help in remembering who was in charge of the storehouse. The One in charge knows all that I don't know. It is He, then, who chooses the food now for this one, now for that, and I have only to pass it on.

Often I have found that what has fed my own soul has fed another, so I will give you the word that was meat in due season to me last night. It was Psalm 119:76 (RV): *Let Thy lovingkindness be for my comfort.*

There are times when the least thing in the world we feel we deserve is comfort, and yet there it is. The everlasting lovingkindness of the Lord our God is ever on its way to comfort us. It is like the love of the father who ran to meet his son. It is like love itself, something that never fails.

❧

January 2

*Let Thy loving Spirit lead me forth into
the land of righteousness.*
Ps. 143:10 (BCP)

When I was a schoolgirl I read James Gall's *Primeval Man Unveiled.* One wonderful day I sat on a stool at the feet of the writer of that book, and asked him to explain things I had not understood. I wondered, as I looked up into the face of that old man, at the loving joy I saw there.

I understand that joy better now. I know that there are few joys so great as to be asked, by one in earnest to understand, what the words one has written mean.

Is it not wonderful to think that we may give joy to the writer of our Book by asking Him to open it to us? We do not think enough of the love of the Spirit of God. Here is a prayer for all who want to enter into the land whose wealth is prepared for us: *Let Thy loving Spirit lead me forth into the land of righteousness.*

May we all be led further and further into that land in this new year.

January 3

Strong consolation.
Heb. 6:18

Everlasting consolation.
2 Thess. 2:16

These two familiar words ring in our hearts like bells. Dr. Way translates "strong consolation" as *all-prevailing encouragement.* And he speaks of the hope of our heart as *an anchor on which our soul rides safely: it cannot slip, it cannot break.*

Everlasting consolation, what a word of joy that is! Some of us are tempted to wonder about the future. We look ahead, and imagine, and fear. For us there is something especially vital in this great thought of consolation that is not for today only, but for endless tomorrows.

Another word was written surely for any of us who are looking beyond the borders of today: Isaiah 26:3–4. *Thou wilt keep him in perfect peace, whose mind* (imagination) *is stayed on Thee: because he trusteth in Thee. Trust ye in the Lord for ever: for in the Lord JEHOVAH is everlasting strength.*

Strong consolation.
Everlasting consolation.
Everlasting strength.

❧

January 4

The vessel that he made of clay was marred in the hand of the potter: so he made it again another vessel, as seemed good to the potter to make it. Cannot I do with you as this potter? saith the Lord. Behold, as the clay is in the potter's hand, so are ye in Mine hand.
Jer. 18:4, 6

When a piece of steel has been subjected to such stress that it has lost its power to recover its elasticity, it is said to be distorted. But it can be made right again. It is put in the furnace, and so it recovers what it had lost.

Perhaps we have given way under the great stress of temptation and become "distorted." Perhaps we have lost hope of ever recovering. "I am like this now; I shall always be like this."

Are we willing to be put into any furnace of God's choosing if only we may be made fit for His use? We cannot choose our furnace. Sometimes it is the *furnace of affliction* of Isaiah 48:10.

But always there is hope. *Cannot I do with you as this potter?* asks the Lord. We are in His hand, and no one can snatch us from His grasp. Our dear Lord says, *My Father, which gave them Me, is greater than all; and no man is able to pluck them out of My Father's hand* (John 10:29).

January 5

Lord, is it I?
Matt. 26:22

One morning, though no one knew it, I felt fretted about something. Before long I came upon another fretted soul, and this startled me, for I seemed to see the very shadow of myself. After that I watched, and I noticed that not only things said and done, but even things thought or felt — lack of faith, courage, peacefulness, happiness, or anything vital — seemed to set a spiritual current flowing. Sooner or later I found that same thing somewhere else, so that when anything went wrong anywhere the question always came, "Lord, is it I?"

Our defeat means loss somewhere else. Our victory means gain. Let us set spiritual currents flowing that will help, not hinder others.

❧

January 6

*And she called the name of the Lord that spake unto her, Thou
God seest me. Thou God of Vision. Wherefore the well was
called The well of Him that liveth and seeth me.
The well of the Life of Vision.
Gen. 16:13–14 (Rotherham margin)*

Thou God seest me, Thou God of Vision. Those words
were spoken by Hagar who had been utterly discouraged but now was encouraged. Sarah had been very unkind to her, but the angel of the Lord did not say to
her, "Poor Hagar!" The sympathy of the Lord our God
is never weakening, it is bracing. Hagar had run away,
so the angel said *Return.* God's love is always brave love.
He never says "Give way"; He always says "Return."

He said more. Perhaps Hagar had thought He did
not care much about her. He cared for Sarah of course,
but *she* was only Hagar. So the angel put her right about
that, and told her how the Lord would bless her, because
He had seen and heard her affliction.

Awed and heartened, Hagar called the name of the
Lord *Thou God seest me, Thou God of Vision.* The well
nearby was named "The well of Him that liveth and
seeth me, the well of the life of vision."

Thank God for that well in the wilderness. If we
are discouraged or tired or hurt today, one long drink
from that well will give us new life, new courage, new
patience to go on running the race set before us — even
to the end.

❧

January 7

I have the keys.
Rev. 1:18

This morning I seemed to see life as a series of rooms, each opening into the next, with all the doors locked between room and room, and all the keys in the Hand that opens, and none shall shut, and that shuts, and none opens (Rev. 3:7).

It seemed to me too that He who had the key of David wrote a word over each door, so that His beloved, looking up and reading, might be prepared for what lay ahead.

We shall never pass through the same room twice. For each one of us our today will tomorrow be that part of eternity which forever lies behind us. It would be terrible to come out as one went in, no richer for all the love that has been poured out on us.

One day the last room will be passed, the last door shut behind us. Then Revelation 4:1 will be our joyful word: "After this I looked, and behold, a door was opened in heaven."

January 8

I will make you fishers of men.
Matt. 4:19

We have toiled all the night, and have taken nothing.
Luke 5:5

We may be tempted to discouragement, if we have toiled all the night and taken nothing that can be brought ashore in a net.

Between Revelation 4 and 11 there is a mysterious story of battle. Sometimes there is defeat, darkness, clash and clamor of spirit. But all through, strung like golden beads on a thread running through the story, there are songs — seven songs, the perfect number. After the seventh song was sung the seventh angel sounded, "and there were great voices in heaven, saying, The kingdoms of this world are become the kingdoms of our Lord, and of His Christ; and He shall reign for ever and ever" (Rev. 11:15).

What will it be when the last of the seven songs is sung and we all join in the song of unimaginable joy, "We give Thee thanks, O Lord God Almighty, which art, and wast, and art to come; because Thou hast taken to Thee Thy great power, and hast reigned" (Rev. 11:17). And we are a week nearer that than we were last week, when we toiled all night and took nothing.

&

January 9

Barnabas . . . when he was come, and had seen the grace of
God, was glad; and he exhorted them all, that
with purpose of heart they would cleave unto the Lord.
Acts 11:23 (RV)

Continue ye in My love.
John 15:9

When Barnabas went to the great, wicked, rich city of Antioch he found people there who had lately turned to our Lord Jesus Christ. He urged the Grecian believers — a little company among tens of thousands of idolaters — to cleave to the Lord, to *continue with* Him.

We may not be able to do much, but we too can do that. We can stay with Him, look to Him, continue with Him. The Greek word used indicates persistent loyalty.

It is the same word used by our Lord Jesus, *Continue ye in My love.* Westcott writes: "The love of Christ is, as it were, the atmosphere in which the disciple lives. It is not something realized at a momentary crisis, but enjoyed continuously. And this enjoyment depends, on the human side, upon the will of man. It can be made the subject of a command."

Listen to that tender, simple word of our Lord Jesus: *"Continue ye in My love.* Don't go away. Stay in My love. I want to have you there. I want to keep you there. Continue ye in My love."

January 10

The grace for light.

There is a lovely old Irish custom called "The grace for light." I read of it in an Irish poem, which tells of a very poor family where that custom was kept. They had no good lamp or lantern, only a tiny rush-light, but when the mother lit it she said: "God be thanked. Now we have a light." And the father replied: "May the Lamb of God lead us all to the Light of Heaven." Then the children were quiet for a moment, and thought of Him "who called us to come and be forgiven."

How good it would be to use the turning on of the electric light as a reminder to say *Thank you* for the blessed gift of light. We cannot have too many of such reminders, for we are by nature forgetful and far too inclined to take all our good things for granted.

But don't let a custom grow into anything formal. Just a *Thank you,* a quick look of love, is enough.

January 11

I thank my God upon every remembrance of you.
Phil. 1:3

Use every remembrance of anyone who loves our Lord as a reminder to look up and thank Him. When the thought of such a one floats through the mind, don't let it merely float. Definitely thank God for that one, and ask for anything known to be needed. If nothing is known, "Do Thou for him" covers all.

There is a good deal about remembering in the Bible, and a good deal about reminders of different kinds. Some of these reminders are like flashes for quickness; others bring a thing gradually to our minds, as the cock crowing caused Peter to "remember gradually" the words of his Lord (Luke 22:61).

The Spirit of God is ready, in His loving way, to bring anyone to mind who needs the help of prayer. If only we are careful not to smother and ignore His soft, reminding whispers, they will come more and more.

January 12

My soul is even as a weaned child.
Ps. 131:2

For when for the time ye ought to be teachers, ye . . . are
become such as have need of milk, and not of strong meat.
Heb. 5:12

The meaning of the Hebrew word translated "weaned" takes us straight to Hebrews 5:12. For "to wean" means "to complete, to ripen," and to be weaned therefore means to be completed, ripened, so that baby food and baby ways are left behind and childish things are put away.

We are not meant to live on prepared food, or to be spoon-fed. God did not mean us always to have the Living Water drawn for us and poured out into glasses and set on our tables. We are meant to *draw water out of the wells of salvation* ourselves (Isa. 12:3). The Eastern picture is not that of turning on a tap, but of going to a well, dipping down into it, and drawing water up for ourselves.

We must not go on being baby souls, starved and thirsty if our food and drink is not doled out to us. Don't let us so live on anything given by others to us. If the time has come for us to be teachers, helpers, givers ourselves, don't let us disappoint our God. He wants His children to be ripened, complete, weaned.

❧

January 13

My lord fighteth the battles of the Lord.
1 Sam. 25:28

Reign in life by One, Jesus Christ.
Rom. 5:17

Don't wait to be attacked. Fight the Lord's battles and He will fight yours. What about that one you know who is being badly tempted? What can you do to help him? Find out a way. Fight the devil who is attacking your brother. Don't slink off and do nothing to help. Fight, fight hard. "Fight the good fight with all thy might."

When the wise Abigail saw David, who at that time was a long way from final victory, she was perfectly sure that he would win because he was fighting the battles of the Lord. The strongest, happiest, most victorious people are those who forget all about themselves in trying to help others. They are fighting the battles of the Lord, and He fights for them and gives them the victory in their own private lives. They reign in life by One, Christ Jesus.

January 14

He riseth from supper, and laid aside His garments; and took a towel, and girded Himself. After that He poureth water into a basin, and began to wash the disciples' feet.... Jesus saith to him [Peter], He that is washed needeth not save to wash his feet, but is clean every whit.
John 13:4–5, 10

Sins are obvious things, but perhaps the dust on the feet means things less easily discerned. That inward uprising of the "I," those lacks of which we are conscious more and more — lacks of love, courage, patience, simple good-tempered contentedness — such lacks make dusty feet.

Is it not blessed and wonderful that He Himself prepared the disciples for the Supper? We may not see the dust distinctly, but He does, and He *poureth water into a basin, and began to wash the disciples' feet.* Wet feet would soon pick up dust again, so He wiped them *with the towel wherewith He was girded.*

Wherever we remember our dear Lord's death, is it not peace to know that He Himself will prepare us? And as the old hymn says,

"When I am clean, Lord, keep me too,
For that is more than I can do."

January 15

*Beloved, if God so loved us, we ought also
to love one another.*
1 John 4:11

Love cannot help loving, any more than water can help flowing. It is pure joy just to love. The love of God follows us wherever we go and whatever we are doing. That we know nothing of it does not matter. That we are wholly occupied in our work does not matter.

I am my Beloved's, and His desire is toward me (Song of Sol. 7:10).

Yea, I have loved thee with an everlasting love (Jer. 31:3).

He will rejoice over thee with joy; He will rest in His love, He will joy over thee with singing (Zeph. 3:17).

Is it not utterly wonderful? He finds pleasure in loving us. To love is the joy of God. And this love, this very love, is the love He sheds abroad in our hearts by the Holy Spirit He has given us (Rom. 5:5).

Is there one of us who would wish to hurt or to ignore love like that?

January 16

The lovers of His Name shall settle down therein.
Ps. 69:36 (Rotherham)

Shall we get into the way of thinking of God's providences* as marginal notes to His written word? Some of us have Bibles with wide margins and it is easy to write a date or a few words which remind us of something He has done, and which we connect with some verse of strength or cheer. But whether we write it or not, His providence is a marginal note on His revealed will, and we shall not go far astray if we read the two together.

The lovers of His Name shall settle down therein is written of His people finding their home in their own land. We are lovers of His Name. Let us settle down in peace as a bird settles down in its nest, not wanting any other nest, not wondering why the wind blows our tree so fiercely sometimes, or why the sky is sometimes dark and the rain falls heavily. All that comes — by the time it touches us — is His holy providence. It will only cause to shine forth more clearly the truth of His words of strong consolation.

---

* Providence…timely care…beneficent care of God. *Concise Oxford Dictionary* (Ed.)

January 17

He setteth an end to darkness.
Job 28:3

These words are spoken of the miner who is searching for precious stones, which are buried in the dark mine. He goes into these dark places and lights them, and so ends the darkness — and he finds the jewels hidden there.

We are here to do that very thing. We have for light the presence and the promises of God. There may be someone whom we are trying to help; we are trying to bring out of the dark mine of that personality precious jewels for our Lord. Perhaps we are terribly tempted to despair, because of continual disappointments and what seems like hopeless weakness of character. But we are not alone. The search, the long effort, is lighted by the presence of our God. He is not baffled by personality. His promises are light.

So let us go on, despairing of no man, for the jewel mine is His. He died to purchase it. *Behold, all souls are Mine* is His word (Ezekiel 18:4).

❧

January 18

*Hold up my goings in Thy paths, that my
footsteps slip not.*
Ps. 17:5

*He maketh my feet like hinds' feet, and setteth me
upon my high places.*
Ps. 18:33

We feel so unlike hinds. But it does not matter how
unlike those beautiful creatures we are, for if by His
grace we walk in His paths He does keep our footsteps
that they slip not. Even a disaster to the flesh only gives
the spirit an opportunity to prove the promises of God.

So let those of us who are well and strong pray
for those who are disabled, that they may be continually *strengthened with all might, according to His glorious
power, unto all patience and longsuffering with joyfulness;
giving thanks unto the Father, which hath made us meet to
be partakers of the inheritance of the saints in light* (Col.
1:11–12).

❧

January 19

*There I will meet with thee, and I will commune
with thee from above the mercy seat.*
Exodus 25:22

I will meet with thee means "meet together by appointment."

Have we ever come late to that appointment? We apologize if we come late to an appointment with a fellow human, especially if he or she has much to do. Should we keep our God waiting? Has He not much to do? *My Father worketh hitherto, and I work,* said His Son who knew (John 5:17).

We cannot imagine the mind that timed the wheeling of the stars thinking little of a few minutes lost in waiting for one who was late at his appointment. If we come to our fixed times of prayer late or unprepared we lose something that cannot be recovered. God help us to be reverent; to be punctual and to be prepared is to be reverent. And then He promises, *I will meet thee* — meet thee by appointment — *and I will commune with thee.*

January 20

In honor preferring one another.
Rom. 12:10

Preferring — this word means "to lead before." To prefer another in honor is to lead another before oneself — to be glad that another can do what one cannot do oneself. It is a word that goes very deep. It cuts straight across the self, the flesh, the I (all three are one really). It asks for something which we cannot do of ourselves. It casts us upon the Strong for strength and the Pure for purity of desire and the great Love of God for love.

We shall have opportunities today to say to the *I* in us, "In the name of the Lord, *go back,*" as in our inward heart and soul we lead another before. Let us refuse to listen to the *I* that clamors within us as we set another before ourself. The Lord help us to live in honor preferring one another.

January 21

Ye ought to help the weak, and to remember the words of the Lord Jesus, how He Himself said, It is more blessed to give than to receive.
Acts 20:35 (RV)

Have you ever wondered who remembered and told St. Paul that lovely word of our Lord, which no one records in the Gospels? We can picture the sorrowful people standing on the shore listening to it, and treasuring it in their hearts.

Paul had been speaking of ordinary work and of working so that we have something to give. But perhaps there was a further thought in his mind. The people wanted to keep him. Others needed him. We are not here to enjoy one another. Love must not be selfish. Love, the truest, deepest kind of love, gives and goes on giving — like the sea upon whose shore they stood together.

It is more blessed (more very happy) to give than to receive. He who knew all kinds of happiness said that. So it must be true. It is true.

❧

January 22

Jesus answered him, . . . The cock shall not crow,
till thou hast denied Me thrice.
John 13:38

Let not your heart be troubled.
John 14:1

After speaking of Peter's fall, which He foresaw, our dear Lord immediately says, *Let not your heart be troubled.* He saw across that day of grief to the restoration that would follow. His eyes were not fixed on the sad interruption to fellowship and joy, but on the hour when Peter would be back in love again, never again to grieve his Lord like that. And so to the surprised and surely greatly troubled little company He said, *Let not your heart be troubled.*

Most of us have things which would naturally greatly trouble us. Let us face these things as our Lord Jesus did in John 13:38 and then go straight on into chapter 14:1.

❧

January 23

*And the children of Israel did so as Joshua commanded, and
took up twelve stones out of the midst of Jordan, as the Lord
spake unto Joshua . . . and carried them over with them
unto the place where they lodged, and laid them down there.
And Joshua set up twelve stones in the midst of Jordan, in
the place where the feet of the priests which
bare the ark of the covenant stood.*
Josh. 4:8–9

One heap of stones was covered over by the waters
of the river; the other heap was set up in the open for
all to see.

Have you passed through some new experience of
the power and the love of your Lord? It helps if you
write the date beside the verse in your Bible which
helped you, or write a word or two of reminder in a
private notebook, lest you forget. That note will be like
the heap of stones set up in the river. Nobody will see it
but your God and you. It is a private heap.

But don't forget the other heap which wasn't private. *Your children shall ask . . . in time to come, saying,
What mean these stones?* (v. 21). The children you look
after, the sick you tend, the people you meet, will notice something that will make them ask questions. Take
them into your confidence. Tell them what has been
done for you, not long ago, but perhaps an hour or two
ago, or yesterday, or last week.

Set up your heap of stones to the glory of your

Lord, so that all will see that He is indeed a God of Deliverances, a splendid, loving, joy-giving Lord whom to serve is the greatest joy in all the world.

January 24

And He took a child, and set him in the midst of them: and when He had taken him in His arms, He said unto them…
Mark 9:36

The little boy might have been shy, standing alone among thirteen grown-up men, perhaps strangers. Most children would be. But there is nothing too small for the love of our Lord Jesus to understand and to remember. Before He spoke words that would naturally cause the men to look at the little boy, thus making him feel observed and uncomfortable, He took him in His arms.

Perhaps this day is going to hold some especially trying things. There are sure to be things that we would not wish to have to face. Before they happen — if we are little enough to let Him do it — our Lord Jesus will do for us just what He did for that child long ago. We need never stand alone among our troubles. We need never be lonely at all. We need never be afraid.

❧

January 25

Ye have need of patience. Heb. 10:36

There are times when great waves of trouble sweep over us, wave upon wave. There are calm times when all goes peacefully, and then suddenly something distressing happens. Satan seems to be having things all his own way. Sometimes those whom we wholly trusted disappoint us terribly, and we are tempted to say, "Whom can I trust?"

But this is fatal. There are many on whom we can count even in the worst times. Let us never look only at the clouds and forget the blue in the sky. There is far more blue than gray.

We are here because we are needed to fight through to victory. We never asked for ease. Well, *this* is not ease, so it is what we expected — not play, but war. It is and always must be a fight of faith. Hebrews 2:9 has a word for us: *We see Jesus…* CROWNED. Nothing can touch that. We follow an undefeated Lord. Love *won* on Calvary.

But we have need of patience. Give us Thy patience, Lord.

January 26

*And Abraham said, My son, God will provide Himself
a lamb for a burnt offering.*
Gen. 22:8

*And Abraham lifted up his eyes, and looked, and behold
behind him a ram caught in a thicket.*
Gen. 22:13

*And Abraham called the name of that place Jehovah-jireh
(margin: The Lord will see or provide).*
Gen. 22:14

In Abraham's sublime faith self was forgotten. The
sacrifice was for the Lord, therefore He would provide.
Isaac was not his but God's. Therefore it was certain that
He would provide for Himself a lamb.

He will provide for Himself, in every work that He
has planned, all that is needed. All things, without a
single exception, are in the hands of our JEHOVAH-JIREH.
Nothing can hinder His purpose.

Sooner or later we shall see what we now by faith
believe. We shall see *the end intended by the Lord,* who is
very pitiful and of tender mercy (James 5:11). We shall
see and we shall sing. Let us sing now.

January 27

Thou therefore, my son, be strong in the grace that is in
Christ Jesus. Thou therefore endure hardness,
as a good soldier of Jesus Christ.
2 Tim. 2:1, 3

From dullness to a friendly word,
From deafness to the song of bird,
From blindness to the birds and flowers
That grow among the rocky hours,
From all that would ungratefully
Becloud my sky, deliver me.

From craven inner selfishness
Whatever be its outward dress,
From fainting when the goal is near,
From faltering in my song of cheer,
From all that is unsoldierly,
Captain of souls, deliver me.

January 28

*And Benaiah . . . went down also and slew a lion
in the midst of a pit in time of snow.*
2 Sam. 23:20

A lion fell into a pit. A man plunged in after him
and slew him. And it was in the time of snow. I have always felt sorry for that lion. Lions detest snow, and that
lion did not have a sporting chance. But his troubles are
over now, and the man has something to teach us.

Benaiah must have been one who had trained himself by many small and private disciplines to be ready for
anything, even a lion in a pit in time of snow. The snow,
of course, made it harder for him too, but he did not
hesitate. He went down and slew the lion.

Quite suddenly in the midst of our ordinary occupations any of us may be face to face with a lion in a pit.
It may be in time of snow — in circumstances which
make it harder than usual to withstand. *But we can.* The
moment we are conscious of the lion (Peter speaks of *the
devil* as a roaring lion in 1 Pet. 5:8), the Spirit of God
will put a sword into our hands. Some strong word of
Scripture will be flashed across our minds. If we grasp
that word, and thrust with all our might, there can only
be one end to the fight. *More than conquerors through
Him that loved us* will tell the end of that lion fight —
even in time of snow.

❧

January 29

*And Moses did look upon all the work, and, behold, they
had done it as the Lord had commanded, even so
had they done it: and Moses blessed them.*
Exod. 39:43

Moses blessed them *after* he saw that all the work
for the tabernacle had been done just as the Lord commanded. He did not give his blessing at the beginning
of the work, for beginnings are easy. Carrying on, and
completing the work perfectly, is much harder. But it is
that which really matters.

I often think of our Lord's words in John 17:4, *I
have finished the work which Thou gavest Me to do.* And
on the cross He said, *It is finished* (John 19:30).

Lord Jesus, who didst finish all for us, hold us faithful to the end, till we too can say, "I have finished the
work which Thou gavest me to do."

❧

January 30

God loveth a cheerful [hilarious] giver. 2 Cor. 9:7

I can do all things through Christ which strengtheneth me.
Phil. 4:13

For it is God which worketh in you both to will
and to do of His good pleasure.
Phil. 2:13

It is not at all easy to be hilarious about certain things. We can give some things so very joyfully that it is easy to be a hilarious giver — there is no effort at all. But it is a different matter where some other things are in question. And yet, who chose what we are to give?

The one vital thing is to let Him choose, and not allow the *I* in us a chance to say anything about it. Then He who loves us best will draw near to us and make His joy our strength. That is the secret of hilarious giving. It is the old word used in another way:

I cannot.

Can God?

God can.

So I can do this thing through Christ who strengthens me. I can; *I will;* for it is God who works in me both to will and to do.

❧

January 31

Array yourselves, then, as God's chosen ones, His consecrated and dearly loved ones, in a heart of sympathy, in kindness, in lowliness, in gentleness, in tireless patience.
Col. 3:12 (Way)

An Australian poet, Adam Lindsay Gordon, who was born more than a hundred years ago, wrote:

> "Life is mostly froth and bubble.
> Two things stand like stone:
> Kindness in another's trouble,
> Courage in your own."

Life is not mostly froth and bubble if you are living for the things that are eternal. But it is perfectly true of the life that has not for its center, Christ.

The last three lines are entirely true. Let us put them into our hearts and minds and live them.

February 1

*And He said, My presence shall go with thee, and I will give
thee rest. And he said unto Him, If Thy presence
go not with me, carry us not up hence.*
Exod. 33:14–15

Let us take these words not so much for a sketch of
unknown months, but just for today. Are they not
wonderful? *If Thy presence go not with me, carry us not
up hence* — for indeed I cannot think of even one hour
without Thee. *My presence shall go with thee* — with thee
through this day. *And I will give thee rest.*

The God of Hope fill us with all joy and peace in
believing that in very truth His presence will go with us
throughout this day.

February 2

God so loved...that He gave...
John 3:16

God so loved that He gave. How much do *you* love? Do you love enough to give — *this?* To each of us there is a different *"this,"* but the question is the same and there can only be one answer, "Let Him take all."

We may be put off from the joy of giving by the thought of the smallness of what we have to offer. But our Lord does not think anything love can give is too small to take. There is nothing small to God; even our little *"this"* matters to Him. When by His loving enabling we look up to Him and say, "Take all — take *this,"* then He comes near and makes peace in our borders and fills us with the finest of the wheat (Ps.147:14). The very Bread of Life empowers us once again.

So now, today, let us so love that we give.

February 3

Thy word is a lamp unto my feet, and a light unto my path.
Ps. 119:105

I have a little transparent picture. When I look at it without the light behind I see nothing. Turn the light on, and there is much to enjoy. John 15:5 covers everything: *Without Me ye can do nothing.* Nothing, not even a little, but simply *nothing.* But the light is there, ready to turn that nothing into something beautiful and radiant.

We do not have to go all the way to the generating station to get light. The light, like the word of our God, is not hidden from us, neither is it far off. Read Deuteronomy 30, verses 12–14. *It is not in heaven, that thou shouldest say, Who shall go up for us to heaven, and bring it unto us?. . . Neither is it beyond the sea, that thou shouldest say, Who shall go over the sea for us, and bring it unto us?. . . But the word* (the light) *is very nigh unto thee.*

Thank God it is "*very* nigh." Without Him who is the Light of the world and of our hearts, we can do nothing, be nothing. But *What nation is there. . . who hath God so nigh unto them, as the Lord our God is in all things that we call upon Him for?* (Deut. 4:7).

❧

February 4

Hard-pressed — yet He humbled Himself,
nor opened His mouth.
Isa. 53:7 (Rotherham)

The assault of our great enemy comes in waves. Sometimes we cannot do the work committed to us to do, and this is indeed a trial of faith. "Hard-pressed" is the word that describes it all.

It is the word spoken of our Lord Jesus in Rotherham's translation. *Hard-pressed — yet He humbled Himself, nor opened His mouth.* To ask why, even to *wonder* why, is to open our mouth. Our Lord Jesus Christ shows us the way here as everywhere. Am I hard-pressed in any direction inward or outward? The only word I speak must be a word of acceptance, "Even so, Father." Underfoot is the rock of Romans 8:28. Overhead is the banner of Eternal Love. Nothing is going wrong, however wrong it seems. All, all is well.

February 5

Create in me a clean heart, O God; and renew
a right spirit within me.
Ps. 51:10

"We can do little things for God. I turn the cake that is frying in the pan for love of Him, and afterwards, if there is nothing else to call me, I prostrate myself in worship before Him who has given me grace to work. Afterwards I rise happier than a king.... It is enough for me to pick up a straw for the love of God." So wrote Brother Lawrence.

Sometimes, when asked to do something we do not want to do, instead of gladness there is gloom. How that must hurt Him, whose love has so tenderly followed our lives from the first day until now. How can we ever have the heart to hurt such love? God forgive us and renew a right spirit within us, and help us from this time forth to pick up our straw, whatever it may be, for the love of God. Not with gloom, but with gladness.

February 6

And I knew that Thou hearest Me always.
John 11:42

When we pray, God always answers. Sometimes He says Yes, sometimes No, sometimes Wait. Let us never talk of unanswered prayers. Our Father *does* answer us when we, His loving children, speak to Him. I think it must sound very strange to Him when we let ourselves use such untrue, ungrateful words. Isn't No an answer? Isn't Wait an answer? Can't we trust our Father if He says No, or Wait?

Our Lord Jesus said *I knew that Thou hearest Me always.* John, who heard Him say that, wrote in his first letter (ch. 5, v. 14) *And this is the confidence that we have in Him, that, if we ask anything according to His will, He heareth us.*

Let us pray, then, in the confidence that He does truly hear and truly answer — always.

February 7

If we suffer, we shall also reign with Him. 2 Tim. 2:12

They which receive abundance of grace and of the gift of righteousness shall reign in life by One, Jesus Christ. Rom. 5:17

In the year 326, Helena, mother of Constantine, went to the Holy Land and found (so it was believed) the three crosses and the nails which were used to crucify our Lord. One of these nails, it is said, was beaten out into a crown and is known as the Iron Crown of Lombardy. This band of iron is "enclosed in a circlet formed of six plates of gold, hinged one to another and richly jeweled and enameled."

We think of a crown as a thing of glory and beauty, but the Crown of Lombardy has another word for us. The iron of suffering and endurance is set within the gold of glory and of beauty.

If we suffer we shall also reign with Him. Have you ever found yourself wishing that it were just a little easier to "reign in life"? And yet that is what each one of us is called to do. God keep us from sinking down to anything less arduous. We were never allured to the Lord's side by a promise of the easy. We never shall be.

In 1668 William Penn wrote a book in prison and called it *No Cross, No Crown.* Everyone knows the name of that book but few have read it. This is from its preface: "Christ's cross is Christ's way to Christ's crown."

❧

February 8

In a great trial of affliction the abundance of their joy
and their deep poverty abounded
unto the riches of their liberality.
2 Cor. 8:2

They have been tested to the uttermost by affliction, yet their
joy has throughout been overbrimming: in spite of their
poverty — their deep poverty — it has overflowed
in a very opulence of unselfishness.
Way

There is something very large and noble about that sort of living. It is the life that never crawls and cringes; it reigns.

What does that mean in our common everyday life? For one thing it means a frankness in owning up, no covering up our faults, no excuses and self-defence, no petty meanness. It means generous thinking about others, not attributing bad motives, not admitting belittling thoughts. It means not only truth and kindness but an all-round "opulence of unselfishness," doing as much as one can to help others (not as little as we can get away with). It means, in a word, a life of love. Love loves to give — not in measure, but abundantly.

February 9

There shall there be a joy of birds. Isa. 35:7 (Septuagint)
I know all the birds of the sky. Ps. 50:11 (Septuagint)

The joy of birds is one of the most wonderful things about them. They seem to sing the moment they awake, even if they are wakened by cold wind and rain. They sing before they set to work to find something to eat. And not one is forgotten by God, who knows all the birds of the sky.

Not one of us is forgotten either; not one of us is overlooked. Not a song we sing is forgotten or overlooked. The God of the joy of the birds wants our joy too.

Some of us cannot sing beautiful songs. Many birds cannot. There is one who can only sing "Pretty dear," and another who only sings "Be quick." But not a bird says, "My song is too small to be worth singing." And He who loves the joy of birds listens.

Because He knows all the birds of the sky He would know if there was one who would not sing, and He would miss that song. Is there one of us whose song He is missing today?

February 10

This day is holy unto our Lord: neither be ye sorry; for the joy
of the Lord is your strength. So the people went forth ... and
made themselves booths ... and sat under the booths. ...
And there was very great gladness.
Neh. 8:10, 16–17

After Nehemiah said *The joy of the Lord is your*
strength, the people suddenly remembered Leviticus
23:39–43: *Ye shall take ... the boughs of goodly trees ... and*
ye shall rejoice before the Lord. That was the commandment, such a happy one. So they gathered branches, and
made booths on their roofs (what fun for the children),
and they sat in these green booths and rejoiced before
the Lord for seven happy days. *And there was very great*
gladness.

Our God will do glorious things if only we let Him
have His way in us. He is a God of Joy, and He loves us
to be happy.

Perhaps one of the secrets of happiness is found in
the very next verse, Nehemiah 8:18: *Also day by day,*
from the first day unto the last day, he read in the book of
the law of God. Can we say with Jeremiah (15:16), *Thy*
word was unto me the joy and rejoicing of my heart: for
truly I am called by Thy Name, O Lord God of Hosts?

❧

February 11

Who can discern his errors? Clear Thou me from hidden
faults. Keep back Thy servant also from presumptuous
sins.... Let the words of my mouth and the meditation of
my heart be acceptable in Thy sight,
O Lord, my Rock and my Redeemer.
Ps. 19:12–14 (RV)

The myrtle plant is small. Its flowers appear insignificant and so do its leaves. But its flowers are really very beautiful, pure white, exquisite under a lens, and of a delicate scent. Its leaves hold a secret. Look through them and you see numbers of small crystal balls; they look like pinpricks in the leaf. Each of these is a little vase of aromatic perfume. Crush the leaf and you will find how sweet it is.

Within each one of us is what the Bible calls "the hidden man of the heart" (1 Pet. 3:4). A glance does not show it, just as a glance does not show what is in the myrtle leaves. But the moment we are carefully regarded, above all when we are tried in any way (crushed as we crush the myrtle leaf), that moment what is there is known. There is no possible way of deception. Courage or cowardice, truth or falsehood, kindness or selfishness, strength or weakness, it is known; and *we* are known for what we really are.

How we need to pray David's prayer in Psalm 19!

❧

February 12

Jesus . . . loved them unto the end.
John 13:1

Then said Jesus, Father, forgive them; for they
know not what they do.
Luke 23:34

If our hearts are full of the love of God, the roughest knocks cannot make us unloving or unpeaceful. But how often, in a moment of impatience, we blame the rough knock! "So-and-so did this; so-and-so said that; my circumstances are difficult. I could be good somewhere else, in some other place or work."

All such excuses are folly. It is not what happens to us but what is *in* us that settles the matter. How often we have to go to our Savior for cleansing and pardon, after some hard knock has caused us to "spill" something unloving which was inside us.

But have we not been comforted by the generous wealth of His pardon? Is it not just like Him to assure us again and again that nothing is changed on His side? He loves us as He did before. He wants us as He did before. His tender mercy embraces us on every side.

Such love draws us back to Calvary. As we think of our own newly discovered sin, we see Him, the sinless One, with new eyes. How did we react towards some trivial, trying touch of people or circumstances? How did He react to the torture of the hammer and the nails?

Father, forgive them; for they know not what they do.
Nothing could surprise anything unloving in Him, for
there was nothing in Him but love.

Is it not wonderful that such a Lord can care for such as
us? Is it not a wonder of wonders that He can want *our* love?

February 13

He measured . . . and He brought me through the waters.
Ezek. 47:3:

When thou passest through the waters, I will be with thee;
and through the rivers, they shall not overflow thee.
Isa. 43:2:

Our waters are shallow because His were deep. In Psalm 69:2 we see what He suffered: *I am come into deep waters, where the floods overflow Me.* For us there is no overflowing: *they shall not overflow thee* is His promise. For Himself those awful depths.

Is there anything we can keep back from such a Savior? O Lord, take our all, our uttermost all; do with us what Thou wilt if only Thy name may be glorified, Thy heart satisfied.

February 14

Thou therefore endure hardness,
as a good soldier of Jesus Christ.
2 Tim. 2:3

"Die hard, my men, die hard!" shouted Col. Inglis to his men as they fought one of the fearful battles of the Peninsular War. Fifteen thousand men were wounded or killed in four hours that day, and the regiment was known as the Die-hards ever after.

Are we die-hards? It is extraordinarily easy to soften. Sometimes we hardly know that we are yielding till some little thing happens that we dislike, and we find ourselves unwilling or unable to go through with it. If this be so, we are not die-hards.

Paul was a die-hard. His whole life and above all his prison letters show that die-hard quality. When he wrote to Timothy *endure hardness*, what he meant was "remain under it." Don't slip from under it. Don't try to shuffle it off. And hardness to him did not mean some trivial little trouble. It meant to suffer *evil.*

How little we know of that. But our Savior knew all that ever could be known, and He endured to the end.

Are we in earnest in wanting to be His die-hards? If so, let us take with confidence His word spoken on the Monday of Passion Week (Matt. 21:22): *And all things, whatsoever ye shall ask in prayer, believing, ye shall receive.*

❧

February 15

He went and preached unto the spirits in prison.
1 Pet. 3:19

For unto this end was the gospel preached even to the dead.
1 Pet. 4:6 (RV)

If the scribes and Pharisees and the rulers of the people could have seen what our Lord was doing on Saturday (their sabbath), how surprised they would have been. No one tells us anything of that day's work except Peter, and no one could have told him of it but our Lord Himself. Was it not just like His love to tell this wonderful secret to the one who had grieved Him? Could He have done anything more comforting than to trust him like that? For truly it was a wonderful secret, and as Peter was allowed to tell it to us we can ponder it and try to understand it.

That day was not spent in rest after the terrible Friday. Our Lord went to the worst of the people who were "in prison," those who had refused to listen to Noah and whose lives had been so wicked that there had to be a Flood. His love went out to them and He hastened to them as soon as He was free from the bonds of the body. And so right on past death we see Him always the same — loving, serving, seeking and saving the lost.

To our Lord, rest was not self-pleasing ease. To serve was His chosen rest.

What about us?

February 16

*And for that the dream was doubled unto Pharaoh; it is
because the thing is established by God, and
God will shortly bring it to pass.*
Gen. 41:32 (RV margin)

But I am poor and needy; yet the Lord thinketh upon me.
Ps. 40:17

When a word from the Lord comes to us twice
about the same time, it is for some special purpose. It
helps and challenges us. What makes the help so vital is
the belief that it did not just "happen," but was planned
by our tender Lord, who knows all about us. It is very
wonderful, and very comforting, to know that He who
has so much to think of is actually *thinking upon me.*

Let us look out for the words which will be "doubled" for us, perhaps today. If we listen we shall hear,
and He whom we love will *put a new song in my mouth,
even praise unto our God: many shall see it* (and hear it)
and fear, and shall trust in the Lord (Ps. 40:3).

❧

February 17

*For this is the will of God, even your sanctification (Greek
hagiasmos, holiness).*
1 Thess. 4:3

God's purpose, in fact, is this, that yours be a consecrated life.
Way

It is the common things of life — not, as we sometimes think, the exceptional things — that offer us
greatest opportunity to live a consecrated life. Zechariah
foresaw the day when our dear Lord is satisfied in His
people and rejoices over them, and he said: *In that day
shall there be upon the bells of the horses, HOLINESS UNTO
THE LORD; and the pots in the Lord's house shall be like
the bowls before the altar. Yea, every pot in Jerusalem and
in Judah shall be holiness unto the Lord of Hosts* (Zech.
14:20–21).

The great thing is to live in the spirit of "holiness
unto the Lord" in all our common things. Is all holy in
my heart? Is all that issues forth in words and in deeds
stamped with the hallmark of holiness?

Search me, O God, and know my heart: try me,
and know my thoughts. Lead me, even me, in the way
of holiness, that my life today may truly be a consecrated life.

February 18

*It was given unto him to make war with the saints,
and to overcome them.*
Rev. 13:7

The words "it was given" are dark with mystery. But there is a light in the darkness: one day that which was given will be taken away.

In the lives of God's children there are sometimes periods when the adversary is "given power to overcome." This power need never touch the spiritual. There the word is the glorious, defiant, Romans 8:37: *In all these things we are more than conquerors through Him that loved us.* But we may be hard pressed, and so I have been praying that our dearest Lord may have the joy of saying about each of us, all of us, "I can count on them for *anything.* I can count on them for peace under any disappointment, under any strain of faith. They will never set limits, saying 'Thus far and no further.' I can trust them up to the hilt."

"Lord, this I wish to be, this I desire, and what Thou seest wanting in me, do Thou, I beseech Thee, vouchsafe to supply."

❧

February 19

The disciple is not above his master: but everyone when he is perfected shall be as his master.
Luke 6:40 (RV)

Luke 6:35 (RV margin): But love your enemies and do them good, and lend, despairing of no man.

Every one when he is perfected shall be as his Master. We look at that assurance and then we think of ourselves and wonder how it can possibly be true for us. Then we look back and find that earlier in the same chapter our Lord told His disciples to despair of no man. He would not have told them that if He Himself could ever despair of anyone.

He will not despair even of us — even of me. *This we also pray for, even your perfecting* (2 Cor. 13:9 RV).

February 20

Have not I commanded thee? Be strong and of a good courage; be not afraid, neither be thou dismayed: for the Lord thy God is with thee whithersoever thou goest. Josh. 1:9

And the priest said, The sword of Goliath the Philistine, whom thou slewest, . . . it is here wrapped in a cloth behind the ephod: if thou wilt take that, take it: for there is no other save that here. And David said, There is none like that; give it me. 1 Sam. 21:9

If our Lord does not despair of us, we must not despair of ourselves. A teacher has no chance with a despairing child, nor has a doctor with a despairing patient. If the child says "I can't" often enough, it simply cannot, and nothing anyone can do can help.

So we must not say, "I can't. Others can, but they are different. It is not in me to conquer. I shall be defeated to the end."

That is folly, and treachery too, for it is disbelieving the word of our God. His word is always, "Fear not; you can." *Have not I commanded thee? Be strong and of a good courage.* Is there one discouraging word in our Bible? Not one.

Try using Bible words as a sword with which to fight the devil of discouragement. *There is none like that; give it me,* David said about the sword of Goliath the Philistine. How much more may we say about the strong word of our God: "There is none like that, O Spirit of the living God. Give it me."

Ask, and He will.

February 21

And blessed is he, whosoever shall not be offended in Me.
Matt. 11:6

All of us are sometimes troubled by questions. Why is the secret of healing not opened more fully? Why is that key not put into wise and loving hands? Why does He whose touch has not lost its ancient power not come immediately and touch and heal? Why have the wicked such awful power? Why are we ourselves sometimes like the little ship on the sea of Galilee beaten by the winds? And even after we have heard our dear Lord's *Peace, be still,* why is it that there is not always instantly a great calm, a lasting calm? Why do the winds return again?

We could go on forever, piling question on question. Why? Why? Why?

But faith is not "trusting God when we understand His ways" — there is no need for faith then. Faith is trusting when nothing is explained. Faith rests under the Unexplained. Faith enters into the deep places of our Lord's words, *And blessed is he, whosoever shall not be offended in Me.* Faith, having entered into those deep places, stays there in peace.

February 22

*Be ye steadfast, unmoveable, always abounding in the work
of the Lord, forasmuch as ye know that your labor
is not in vain in the Lord.*
1 Cor. 15:58

The king of Egypt who tried to do most for his people, and utterly failed, was the last of his dynasty (the 18th dynasty). He died in 1350 B.C. cursed by his people, and his palace was abandoned and the records of his reign were flung on a rubbish heap and left there as worthless.

Hundreds of years later this old rubbish heap was found. When the records were read, much that had been laughed at in the Bible as "impossible" was proved to be true, for there were allusions to those very things in these records.

So God used "a failure" to help to do one of the greatest things that can be done — establish faith in His Book. That king, Akh Naten, was His servant, and He never wastes the lives of His servants. Their very failures are gathered up and used.

Even when we feel we have failed, God writes *Not in vain* over everything we have tried to do in His name.

❧

February 23

And he comforted them, and spake to their hearts.
Gen. 50:21 (margin)

Joseph spoke kindly to his brothers; he spoke to their hearts.

Everyone has a chance to do this. If something upsetting happens, don't let it upset. But if it has, "speak to the heart" of the one who is causing the upset. Find the heart concealed under the outside upset part, and speak to it. A tired heart confuses the mind, and so also the outlook on life.

Even in the most difficult days it is not hard to find the heart of a fellow-lover of our Lord Jesus. Find it, and then, taking as little notice as possible of the outside, *speak to the heart.*

February 24

Thou wilt keep him in perfect peace, whose mind is stayed on Thee: because he trusteth in Thee. Trust ye in the Lord for ever: for in the Lord JEHOVAH is everlasting strength.
Isa. 26:3–4

The King James Version margin gives "imagination" as the meaning of the word "mind." The present moment rarely troubles us. It is when we let ourselves imagine what may be lying ahead that we find ourselves, often, shaken or anxious or cowardly.

Did you ever notice that you never stand up to anything hard in a dream? You invariably either succumb or wake up. As a child I read *Foxe's Book of Martyrs* and dreamt dreadful Spanish Inquisition dreams. It was the greatest grief to me that I never stood the torture but always escaped it somehow. Either I gave in or I woke up. I thought it meant that if I had lived in those awful days I would have denied the Lord. For years this unspoken fear haunted me, till at last I understood that the grace of God is not given to us for dreams, creations of our imagination. The grace of God is given us for real life.

He who strengthens and illuminates our today will make strong and radiant our tomorrow. This must be true, for with Him is no variableness, "neither shadow that is cast by turning," as James 1:17 (RV) tells us for our comfort. Therefore let us stay our imagination on Him and refuse to let it wander off into unknown tomorrows.

Trust ye in the Lord for ever. Him we know — for *I know whom I have believed, and am persuaded that He is able to keep that which I have committed unto Him* (2 Tim. 1:12). To Him I have committed my future, my tomorrow. I may safely trust Him, *for in the Lord JEHOVAH is everlasting strength.*

February 25

Then said Agrippa unto Festus, This man might have been set at liberty, if he had not appealed unto Caesar.
Acts 26:32

It is a mistake to talk much or think much about one's temptations. Paul was human, so he must have been tempted when he heard that he could have been set free *if* he had not appealed to Caesar. But never once does he refer to that private temptation.

To talk about one's temptations is to emphasize them. The better way is to look up from them to our Lord, who can and does give us victory over them.

Because he did this, Paul had "a heart at leisure from itself" to help others — to help us.

❧

February 26

A thorn in the flesh, the messenger of Satan. 2 Cor. 12:7

The Lord said unto Satan, Behold, all that he hath is in thy power. Job 1:12

[Satan said,] Put forth Thine hand now. Job 2:5

And the Lord said unto Satan, Behold he is in thine hand. Job 2:6

So Satan . . . smote Job. Job 2:7

This is your hour, and the power of darkness. Luke 22:53

There was given to me a thorn in the flesh. 2 Cor. 12:7

When He hath tried me, I shall come forth as gold. Job 23:10

Father, if Thou be willing . . . nevertheless not My will, but Thine, be done. Luke 22:42

As a child I puzzled over the fact that though all Christian people spoke of pain as sent from God, they did all that in them lay to avoid it, or if it came, to get rid of it. Doctors who helped them to do so were prayed for as very special servants of God. And yet they were working against the very thing that God had sent.

It was all very puzzling, and I can remember the delight of finding the words, *An enemy hath done this* (Matt. 13:28), and feeling that they must apply to all that hurt and wounded either spirit or body. And yet there was a mystery somewhere. And it was not explained.

I think now that it never will be explained until we stand in the light of God; but these words from Paul and Job and our Lord's own prayer help us to understand.

All pain, all ill, is a messenger from Satan, and yet the thorn was a gift. The Spirit of God takes care to let us know that it was Satan's hand, not the Father's, that hurt Job. And yet that cruel hand was turned into a crucible, and the fire refined the gold. The power of darkness crucified the Lord of glory. But Love won on Calvary.

❧

February 27

I am become like a bottle in the smoke; yet do I not forget Thy statutes.   Ps. 119:83

Although the fig tree shall not blossom, neither shall fruit be in the vine, . . . yet, I will rejoice in the Lord, I will joy in the God of my salvation.   Hab. 3:17–18

But I will hope continually, and will yet praise Thee more and more.   Ps. 71:14

Do you know what it is to go to your Bible desperate for something specially sustaining and reviving? That was how I opened mine this morning — and this is what I got: Psalm 119:83, *I am become like a bottle in the smoke.* I saw that bottle, that dried-up old goatskin hung up in the smoke. It was exactly what I felt like at that moment and I could not see how it was going to help me at all.

Yet do I not forget Thy statutes. That "yet" (though not in the Hebrew) suddenly took me to other "yets" and "buts," those great words of faith that swing us round from looking at smoky bottles to look at things eternal (which smoky bottles are not). First Habakkuk's dauntless *Yet will I rejoice* when everything had gone wrong; then in the Psalms *I will hope continually, and will yet praise Thee more and more.* "Yet" means "increase, continue, carry on" — in joy and praise.

So let us defy the devil who loves to make us feel smoky, and "increase and continue" in the glorious joy of the Lord that is strength.

February 28

The Lord is on my side; I will not fear:
what can man do unto me?
Ps. 118:6

When He giveth quietness, who then can make trouble?
Job 34:29

The Lord is for me (margin). *What can man do unto me?* Nothing. Nothing that really matters. Nothing that can do any harm. Nothing that will not be turned to golden good.

Sometimes we feel as though man could do a great deal. A perverse child can cloud a whole day. The sight of deadly sin, injustice and suffering can overwhelm us. And deeper things, the inward assaults of the never-resting foe (though he is not man but stronger than man) can seem to do appalling things.

But still the word stands, the question that can have only one answer. *The Lord is for me. What can man do unto me?* Nothing.

And to another question there is only one answer. *When He giveth quietness, who then can make trouble?* No one.

However things seem, the answers to those two questions are among the things that cannot be shaken.

February 29

Wherefore putting away lying, speak every man truth with his neighbor: for we are members one of another.
Eph. 4:25

All the different translations bring out clearly the "for" of Ephesians 4:25. Not, "That we may be united, let us be truthful with one another" — which would be a natural and sensible way to put it — but *because* "we are as it were parts of one another" (Weymouth), let us be sincere.

This sort of sincerity is searching, but it leads straight to the most restful thing in all the world: perfect confidence in one another.

March 1

He that shall endure unto the end, the same shall be saved.
Matt. 24:13

He that shall endure unto the end — those words come three times in the Gospels. In Hebrews 3:6 and 14 we have *firm unto the end, steadfast unto the end,* and twice the thought of hope is linked up with the word. *If we hold fast the confidence and the rejoicing of the hope firm unto the end,* and *The full assurance of hope unto the end* (Heb. 6:11).

How much easier it would be if we knew when hearts that are holding out against the Lord would yield, or when some private trial of our own would pass. It was like that in Bible days; there was the same temptation to tire in hope and to fail in the joy of hope, to weaken and get slack. So we have those glorious, strong words in the Gospels and in Hebrews, and there is another that is sheer joy — 1 Corinthians 1:8: *Our Lord Jesus Christ, who will also keep you steadfast to the very end* (Weymouth).

So we can turn Jude 24–25 into praise and thanksgiving. "Now unto Him that is able to keep us from falling and to present us faultless before the presence of His glory with exceeding joy…be glory and majesty, dominion and power, both now and ever. Amen."

March 2

*Converse with one another in the music of psalms, in hymns
and songs of the spiritual life, praise the Lord heartily with
words and music, and render thanks to God the Father
in the Name of our Lord Jesus Christ
at all times and for all things.*
Eph. 5:19 (Moffatt)

*Singing and striking the strings with your heart
unto the Lord.*
(Rotherham)

When I was small I used to think that, if I wanted
very much to do a thing, that thing was probably wrong.
And if I didn't want to do it, it was probably right.

That is not quite fair to God, for *His commandments are not grievous,* not heavy and burdensome (1
John 5:3).

It is worthwhile to look out for the words in the
Bible that tell us to do pleasant things, like singing.
Psalm 71:23 says: *My lips shall greatly rejoice when I sing
unto Thee; and my soul, which Thou hast redeemed.* How
true that is; which of us does not know it? The way of
escape from the wilderness (see Psalm 63, the wilderness
psalm) is by the way of praise and song.

❧

March 3

Whom have I in heaven but Thee? and there is none upon earth that I desire beside Thee.
Ps. 73:25

We all know the hymn "Jesus, Lover of my soul." The line "Thou, O Christ, art all I want," comes to us with searching power. It is strangely easy to want Him and a great many other things too. We want to do what we want to do, and to be where we want to be. This is not desiring Christ our Lord and His will only. It is not, "Thou, O Christ, art ALL I want."

Our Lord wants us to come to the place where we can truly say with David that there is no one and nothing on earth that we desire beside Him. David goes on in the next verse, *My flesh and my heart faileth,* and that is often our experience too. But David does not stop there, and neither need we. He ends with a triumphant *But God.* Verse 26: *But God is the strength of my heart, and my portion for ever.*

"Thou, O Christ, art all I want;
More than all in Thee I find."

March 4

I watch, and am as a sparrow alone upon the house top.
Ps. 102:7

The man who wrote that must have known sparrows well. A sparrow alone would indeed be a lonely bird. Who can read those words without seeing that solitariness of the soul which all of us by nature most dread?

Surely the Spirit guided the sequence of the Psalms, for the next, Psalm 103, opens a certain and glorious way of escape for that sparrow on the house top. Fly into that air and there is instant deliverance from that which gives loneliness its power to crush and weaken.

There is a sense in which every soul that follows hard after its God must find itself alone. "He who follows Him the nearest needs must walk alone." It is part of the discipline of life. It is not explained.

Let us rest our hearts on our Lord's words about the sparrows, not one of whom, not even the one on the house top, is unregarded. Luke 12:6–7: *Are not five sparrows sold for two farthings, and not one of them is forgotten before God?. . . Fear not therefore: ye are of more value than many sparrows.*

Bless the Lord, O my soul: and all that is within me, bless His holy Name. Let us find our way quickly into the life and liberty of Psalm 103.

March 5

In a place of green grass, there He has made me dwell.
Ps. 23:2 (Septuagint)

Have you ever felt discouraged in prayer because words would not come? Often our Lord Jesus turned Bible words into prayer. The Psalm book was the prayer book of the early Church. It is ours still. We cannot ever fathom the depths of this book.

Bishop Moule said that a hymnbook was a good prayer book, too. Real hymns, like real songs, are born only when the soul is very near God. This is why they have power to help. They offer words to us when we have none of our own.

Thank God for our hymns and songs and books. Above all, thank God for His Book of books. Is there a need it cannot meet? Is there a dryness it cannot refresh? Not one. *In a place of green grass, there He has made me dwell.*

March 6

Thou art worthy, O Lord, to receive glory and honor and power: for Thou hast created all things, and for Thy pleasure they are and were created.
Rev. 4:11:

We would be astonished if the one appointed to lead a meeting or a service came without preparation. But what about us? Is it not our worship too? We know how a single note dropped out of a chord in music is a loss to the chord. If one lover of the Lord goes to a meeting unready, conscious perhaps of some shadow of self in the center, some out-of-tuneness, there will be loss to everyone.

Take time to prepare. 1 John 1:7, or John 13:5, or any words the Spirit brings to mind can work effectively in a very short time. If only all who love our dear Lord are ready to answer the call, "O come, let us adore Him," then there will be pure worship, pure adoration.

March 7

By Myself have I sworn, saith the Lord, for because thou hast done this thing. . . in blessing I will bless thee.
Gen. 22:16–17

Let us set ourselves to obey God today. Whether the thing He asks of us is great, or so small that we would be ashamed to let anyone know that it cost us anything, let us yield it to him as obediently as Abraham yielded Isaac.

The way of obedience is the way of joy. It leads to a blessing that is beyond our understanding, even as the blessing of Genesis 22:17–18 was beyond Abraham's. It results in blessing for others as well as ourselves.

Is there any word of my Lord to me which I am refusing to obey? Perhaps I am arguing about it, or trying to smother and forget it, because I do not want to obey. Obey it — then *In blessing I will bless thee* is His promise.

March 8

Therefore now go, lead the people unto the place
of which I have spoken unto thee: behold,
Mine Angel shall go before thee.
Exod. 32:34

These words are taken from the story of Israel's sin.
I am glad that we may take part of a verse and use it. The
New Testament writers did this when they quoted the
Old, and our Lord did it too. These words from verse
34 have something very strengthening and comforting
for us, as we try to help others to find the way Home.

We don't go out alone into any endeavor. As we talk
with anyone, anywhere, One whom we do not see but
who is truly there goes before us. His Presence guides
our poor endeavors, and makes the little that we do ef-
fective, though perhaps we do not see that it is so.

Thank God for the Angel of His Presence who goes
before us today.

❧

March 9

Sing unto the Lord with thanksgiving; sing praise upon the
harp unto our God: who covereth the heaven with clouds,
who prepareth rain for the earth, who maketh grass
to grow upon the mountains.
Ps. 147:7–8

The Septuagint version is *Begin the song with thanks-giving.* "God's weather never spoiled God's work," C. A. Fox used to say at Keswick when the rain pattered on the tent and the voice of the speaker could not be heard. Don't wish for anything that isn't. Whatever our clouds and rain may be, whatever form they take, let us see God's hand behind the scene. *He* waters the mountains. The clouds and the rain do not come of themselves.

Whether it is rain or sunshine for us today, let us *begin our song with thanksgiving.*

❧

March 10

And the Lord answered . . . with good words and comfortable words.
Zech. 1:13

In the second year of Darius Hystaspes, "exactly five months after the building of the temple had been resumed" (see Hag. 1:13–15) and two months after the last promise God gave through Haggai to the people that He would overthrow the kingdoms (Hag. 2:20, 22), the prophet Zechariah saw in a vision a rider upon a red horse "in a myrtle bush," and One whom he calls the Angel of the Lord (our Lord Jesus Christ) standing among the myrtle bushes. Read Zechariah 1, verse 8 onwards.

He also sees an angel who interprets the vision to him. Behind the rider on the red horse were other riders, and they tell the rider that the world is quiet. But God had promised that in a little while He would shake the heavens and the earth, and the Desire of all nations would come (Hag. 2:6–7). Now the riders say that nothing of the sort is happening.

Have we not often been as perplexed as the riders were, as we thought of some promise apparently unfulfilled? But our Lord shows us the way of peace. He "answered and said, O Lord of Hosts." He did not answer the riders, or the man on the red horse. He turned to His Father, just as He did in that last evening before

His crucifixion. And then among the myrtle trees were spoken good words and comfortable words.

If we are to go through our difficult times in peace, unweakened in hope, we must do what our Lord Jesus did when the riders brought their report. Let us turn to our Father. Then, though our questions may not be answered (there was no answer to His *How long?*), we shall surely hear in the depths of our hearts good and comfortable words.

❧

March 11

What man is there of you, whom if his son ask bread,
will he give him a stone?
Matt. 7:9

If ye then, being evil, know how to give good gifts unto your
children, how much more shall your Father which is in
heaven give good things to them that ask Him?
Matt. 7:11

The God of Jacob; which turned the rock into a standing
water, the flint into a fountain of waters.
Ps. 114:7–8

Often our prayers are not answered according to our desires. Our Lord said that no loving father would give his child a stone when he asked for bread, but sometimes what we are given looks like a stone.

But what a stone it is! It is a rock which our God turns into a pool, a flint that becomes a fountain.

If we seem to receive a stone when we pray today, let us rejoice, for we know the blessed secret of the rock and the flint.

March 12

I will put up with you.
Isa. 46:4 (Septuagint margin)

Beloved, if God so loved us, we ought also
to love one another.
1 John 4:11

Do you sometimes say in your heart, "So-and-so is very hard to put up with?" If God puts up with us we ought also to put up with one another. If God is not hard on us, we ought not to be hard on one another. Think of the patience of God with us who so often try His patience. That thought helps us to be patient with others.

Another help is to think of the good qualities of those who try us. There is always good to find. Look for it. Think of it. Dwell on it rather than on the opposite. This is what our dear Lord did. *"They have kept Thy word,"* He said to His Father, overlooking so much.

Do we speak good of others, as He spoke good of the disciples who so often disappointed Him? *If God so loved us, we ought also to love one another.*

March 13

Come unto Me, all ye that labor and are heavy laden,
and I will give you rest.
Matt. 11:28

For he that is entered into his rest, he also hath ceased from
his own works. . . . Let us labor therefore
to enter into that rest.
Heb. 4:10–11

Labor in Hebrews 4:11 means "make haste." Is the word used to remind us that we shall not drift into rest? There must be the will to enter in. Perhaps what demands most will power is the resolution to cease from our own works, our own busyness, and to stay our minds upon our God.

We pray, and the answer is not what we expect. It seems an answer of loss, and sometimes loss upon loss. We must cease from our own thoughts about it and believe that what He has allowed is the perfect answer for the moment. As we believe, and accept, we enter into rest and the sense of strain passes into peace.

This covers all life: the illness of those we love, mental or spiritual suffering, the unexplained, everything. Let us not lose one hour in needless ineffective distress. Let us hasten by an act of the will to come to Him for rest.

March 14

Hold fast the form of sound words.
2 Tim. 1:13

God's love is very brave. He trusts us not to look back and wonder about things, or wonder about present things either, or fear for future things. Often in our work for Him something happens which seems the most hindering thing possible. It cuts straight across our hopes and plans. The only thing to do then is to take 2 Timothy 1:12 and use it about everything.

I know whom I have believed, and am persuaded that He is able to keep that which I have committed unto Him.

If we are certain, beyond a doubt, that He whom we have believed is able to keep that precious thing or person which we have committed unto Him, then we have peace. If we hold fast the form of these sound words, they will carry us through any storm. They will lead us straight to those other words in Isaiah 26:3: *Thou wilt keep him in perfect peace, whose mind is stayed on Thee: because he trusteth in Thee.*

❧

March 15

Jesus answered and said unto him, If a man love Me,
he will keep My words.
John 14:23

For this is the love of God, that we keep His commandments:
and His commandments are not grievous.
1 John 5:3

In my room is a little cabinet full of letters from my children. When I have to ask one of them to do a hard thing I don't go and look through the letters to find the one which is most loving. Words are not the proof of love. They are the fragrance of the flower of love, but they are not the flower, nor even the proof that there is a flower, for fragrance can be imitated. "Judas kissed Him much." Our Lord Jesus gives us the one unfailing test of love: *If a man love Me he will keep My words.*

The Lord help us to give Him the joy that our children give to us when they loyally and lovingly keep our words. Let us give Him this joy today.

March 16

He hath made everything beautiful in its time:
also He hath set eternity in their heart.
Eccles. 3:11 *(RV margin)*

The book of Ecclesiastes does not show the life of a child of God. Never let us live in that sad book. There are a few happy verses in it, but on the whole it is sad because it is a true description of life *under the sun,* and if our life is *hid with Christ in God* (Col. 3:3) it is not lived *under the sun* but far above the sun.

There is a wonderful word even in this sad book. *He hath made everything beautiful. . . . He hath set eternity in their heart* — the heart of all beautiful things.

What do you think that means?

❧

March 17

Seek the Lord, and His strength: seek His face evermore.
Ps. 105:4

The first words of Psalm 105 are jubilant commands that, when all goes well with us, seem so gloriously easy to obey. It would be hard to do anything else. But the Spirit knew that there would be different hours, hours when the natural foundations of courage, hope, peace and joy would be quicksand under our feet. And so He pauses, as it were, to remind us of our Strength, the Rock of our hearts. Seek *His* face.

Julian of Norwich wrote that when we reach heaven, "Then shall none of us be stirred to say: *Lord, if it had been thus, then it had been full well:* but we shall all say with one voice: *Lord, blessed mayest Thou be, for it is thus: it is well.* Moreover He that shall be our bliss when we are there is our Keeper while we are here; and the last word of revelation is the same as the first: Thou shalt not be overcome. He said not: *Thou shalt not be tempested, thou shalt not be travailed, thou shalt not be distressed;* but He said: *Thou shalt not be overcome.*"

March 18

I go away, and come again unto you.
John 14:28

These words refer to the parting, before our Lord Jesus would come again and receive His disciples unto Himself, never to be parted from Him again.

But can one thought, however rich, ever exhaust the meaning in His words? These special words, *I go away, and come again unto you,* cast light on Isaiah 48:21: *"They thirsted not when He led them through the deserts."* He who never really leaves us does at times appear to do so. We all know what desert times are, what it means *not* to see Him clearly, *not* to hear His voice, *not* to feel His presence.

But "there is not enough darkness in all the world to put out the light of one little glowworm." This word of cheer is far more unquenchable than any light of earth. Does it seem as though He has gone away? He has not, but does it sometimes seem so? Then let His word do its loving will in our hearts. "I will not stay away. I go away, *and come again unto you.*"

March 19

And the Lord said, Simon, Simon, behold, Satan hath de-
sired to have you, that he may sift you as wheat: but I have
prayed for thee, that thy faith fail not.
Luke 22:31–32

Our Lord Jesus prayed for Peter that his faith might
not fail, and within a few hours his courage did fail.

The more we think of those last hours of our Lord,
just before Calvary, the more we see every kind of trial
compressed into them. It was not only that His cup was
filled to overflowing with suffering, but that every vari-
ety of suffering was there. It is easy to escape from the
intolerable thought of such suffering by saying He was
God, and so where Peter was concerned He looked forward to the victory that would be given. But we know,
though we cannot understand it, that He was man too,
and Hebrews 2:18 says that He *suffered* being tempted.

Is there one for whom we are praying, who seems
to be unhelped by our prayer? Are we suffering the bitterness of disappointment? Our dear Lord has been this
way before us. He who turned and looked upon Peter
(Luke 22:61) will give to us, will *maintain* in us, His
own tenderness of spirit, the love that cannot be tired
out of loving, the patience that will not let go.

March 20

None of his steps shall slide.
Ps. 37:31

Thou hast enlarged my steps under me,
that my ankles did not slip.
Ps. 18:36 (margin)

Ye shall be betrayed . . . and some of you shall they cause
to be put to death. . . . But there shall not
an hair of your head perish.
Luke 21:16–18

These words of our God are most gloriously trustful. Our Lord was speaking to some who were to die by martyrdom and He said in effect: "I trust you not to misunderstand when your ankles do slip and every hair of your head does perish. I trust you never to be offended in Me."

There is a delightful "though" in Psalm 37:24 which goes to the core of the matter. *Though he fall, he shall not be utterly cast down: for the Lord upholdeth him with His hand.* Kay translates it, *He shall not be prostrated, for the Lord supports his hand;* and Rotherham, with enchanting vigor: *Though he fall, he shall not be hurled headlong, for the Lord is holding his hand.*

What do falls matter if the Lord is holding us up? He will keep us safe; we shall be more than conquerors through Him who loves us.

March 21

Thinkest thou that I cannot beseech My Father, and He shall
even now send Me more than twelve legions of angels?
Matt. 26:53 (RV)

The silver is Mine, and the gold is Mine,
saith the Lord of Hosts.
Hag. 2:8

A legion was a company of 6,000 soldiers. Does our Lord need *our* service? A word from Him to His Father would, He said, bring more than twelve legions of angels, more than 72,000 to help Him. Think of the stars; we never with our naked eyes see more than about 2,000 at a time. Try to imagine a host of 72,000, each one fit to offer perfect service. Why should the Lord of all the angels want you and me at all?

Does our Lord need our gifts? Before the mountains or plains were settled, where the gold and silver and copper are hidden, there He was. It was the Lord of Hosts, the hosts of the angels, who said, *The silver is Mine, and the gold is Mine.* All powers, all possessions are His. Why should He want anything that we can give?

"Treasure in heaven" answers that question. He has gone to prepare a place for us (John 14:2). He does not want it to be empty, but full of treasure for us. Such is His love that He loves us to give cheerfully that which will fill the place He is preparing for us, full of unimaginable treasure. What a Lord!

❧

March 22

Will a man rob God? Yet ye have robbed Me. But ye say,
Wherein have we robbed Thee? In tithes and offerings.
Mal. 3:8

Tithes and offerings are not the same. "Tithes *and* offerings," God says. In writing to the converts in Corinth (2 Cor. 9:6–11), Paul does not speak of tithes; he takes them for granted. He speaks of offerings which are over and above tithes.

Love always finds ways to do more than give tithes. It gives free-will offerings, something over and above what must be given. That is the joy of love. It is about such love, and the things such love does, that God says "his righteousness remains for ever" (v. 9). He calls our little love-gifts by that great name, and lays them up as treasure in heaven.

Are we faithful in our tithes? Are we loving in our offerings?

March 23

Search me, O God, and know my heart: try me, and know my thoughts: and see if there be any wicked way in me, and lead me in the way everlasting. Ps. 139:23–24

Sometimes we are conscious of something wrong. We feel in ourselves a grumbling spirit, or an unloving spirit, or the petulant, arguing spirit that asks Why? We honestly want victory, and yet it does not come.

Perhaps these words from the preface to *The Spirit of Discipline* by Bishop Paget can help us:

> The grace of God may be turned at a particular time to a particular task, but its true place is at the center not the circumference of life. Our failure, even if we have really tried to conquer a special sin, may be because of a lack of desire, or will, or watchfulness in other directions far removed, perhaps, in apparent character and sphere from that particular trial in which defeat and discouragement is undergone.
>
> For instance, it is not strange that moods of sullenness should brood relentlessly over the heart that though it hates its own gloom is not prepared to forgive wholly some bygone wrong; it is not strange that tempers should be uncertain when appetites are undisciplined. We cannot tell where the soul may find itself betrayed *if anywhere, at any point of its defence, the will is treacherous.* For the spiritual combat is one; and the Spirit of Discipline comes to sanctify us wholly; and *to desire victory at one point while we are contentedly failing at another may be to court disaster and repulse at both.*

March 24

And Moses returned unto the Lord, and said, Oh, this people have sinned a great sin, and have made them gods of gold. Yet now, if Thou wilt forgive their sin —; and if not, blot me, I pray thee, out of Thy book which Thou hast written.
Exod. 32:31–32

The love in Moses' words smites us. *That* is the way we must look on the sins and weaknesses of others, not condoning (Moses did not condone), but with eyes of uttermost love.

God's word to Moses in verse 34 was *Now go, lead the people.* Don't give them up as hopeless. God would deal with the sin; it would not be overlooked. But even so, Moses was not to despair of them. Instead, *Now go, lead the people unto the place of which I have spoken unto thee.*

The Lord give to us all Moses' love, Christ's love, the love that loves the disappointing — not the lovables only, but the unlovables.

≈

March 25

*So He led them through the depths, as through the
wilderness. Ps. 106:9*

"Led" means there *"caused to go on."* We all want to
go on, not through the shallows but through the depths
of prayer. The "burro" or wild donkey of the Mexican
deserts digs and digs in the sand until it finds water. It
invariably does. What our wonderful God can do for
His donkeys in the natural world He can do for those of
us who are just that in the spiritual.

I have found that to let oneself wander far at other
times is what most surely leads to wandering thoughts in
prayer. Instead, let us allow all sorts of things to act as reminders, as calls to prayer. For example, once when held
up by traffic on the road, the friend with me talked of
someone who was lonely; thereafter, to be held up on the
roads reminded me to pray for the lonely of the earth.

Then there is the flash of memory. A name, place,
person, or something seen or heard or read flashes for
one second across the mind. It can be lost or turned to
prayer; the choice is with us.

As we go on practicing prayer in this simple way we
can trust that He who caused His people to go through
the depths as through an open wilderness will cause us
also to go through these deeper places of prayer. The
patient Spirit will help us in our weakness, for though
we do not know how to pray as we ought He Himself
prays for us (Rom. 8:26).

March 26

Ye are they which have continued with Me
in My temptations.
Luke 22:28

A lover of our Lord was asked which of all His words she would most wish to hear Him say to her. She answered: *"Ye are they which have continued with Me in My temptations."*

From time to time most of us have to do with souls who are distressed beyond measure because of thorns in the path. They are surprised to find them there. They seem to think of thorns as belonging to the crown of the Crucified, not to the path of His followers. "Think it not strange": they think it very strange.

What can we do to help them? If only Calvary be the background of our living, if only we continue with our Lord in Gethsemane, if only every common word and deed, our whole bearing, our whole being is steeped in the spirit that was His when He set His face steadfastly to go to Jerusalem, then those who look to us will see that cross and be drawn into that fellowship. There is no other way to help them. There is no other way to be helped ourselves.

March 27

I am crucified with Christ: nevertheless I live; yet not I, but
Christ liveth in me: and the life which I now live in the flesh
I live by the faith of the Son of God, who loved me,
and gave Himself for me.
Gal. 2:20

During the war, the Victoria Cross was awarded to
Lt. Jackman posthumously. "He was killed while still
inspiring everyone with the greatest confidence by his
bearing."

May it be so with us. Let us die while still inspiring
everybody. Make us inspirers of others to the very end.

If we are to be that, we must first be inspired ourselves. Galatians 2:20 tells us how, but only the Spirit
of God can open to us the meaning of these words. Let
us read them over in His presence, giving Him time to
cause them to speak to us in the depths of our hearts.

March 28

Set to Lilies, a testimony. Ps. 80 Title (RV margin)

Cause Thy face to shine; and we shall be saved.
Ps. 80:3, 7, 19

Isn't the Bible amazing? Continually things that differ are bound together as by golden chains. *The altar of God . . . God my exceeding joy* (Ps. 43:4). *When the burnt offering began, the song of the Lord began also* (2 Chron. 29:27). *The soldiers platted a crown of thorns, and put it on His head. . . . Thou settest a crown of fine gold on His head* (John 19:2 and Ps. 21:3, RV). And so it continues from Genesis to Revelation.

Perhaps the title to Psalm 80 explains it. *Set to Lilies, a testimony.* The lily breaks through hard ground after rain. Psalm 80 is hard ground. It is full of the hardness of suffering with others or for others; sin is the cause of that suffering.

But look at the lilies. Three times they break through the hardness of that pain with a sudden hope and joy. *Cause Thy face to shine and we shall be saved.* There is no selfishness here: it is not *I*, but *we* shall be saved.

Whatever form our hard ground may take at the moment, let us rejoice in our lilies and listen to their testimony. There is an end set to pain, to sin. The day will come, and we shall see it, when the word will be, *Neither shall there be any more pain* (Rev. 21:4).

March 29

Speak out your thoughts to each other in psalms, in hymns, in chants inspired by the Holy Spirit.
Eph. 5:19 (Way)

One of the chief joys of friendship is the sense of being understood. You are free to think aloud, you do not need to be careful. If there is an inner inhibition, "Be careful how you speak, how you write; it may be misunderstood," then there is an utter end of this most restful element in friendship.

Paul lifts this truth to the spiritual plane. Our life of song is as certain to be attacked as our life of prayer, of which it is indeed a part. For it is precious, and all precious things are attacked.

So we need to come prepared in spirit before meeting to sing. Then when the enemy prowls about he will find great wings folded round us, and the presence of the Lord in our midst.

March 30

Awake, O north wind; and come, thou south; blow upon my garden, that the spices thereof may flow out.
Song of Sol. 4:16

There are two pots of lilies in my room. In one the flowers are large and perfect; in the other the bloom has missed something. It does not touch perfection.

A glance discovers the reason. Its leaves are dusty.

Awake, O north wind — sharp, cold, unwelcome — *and come, thou south* — welcome by all — *blow upon my garden.* Round about us day by day these winds blow. They breathe the very breath of life upon us, for they come at the call of Him who is our Breath of Life.

Are we receiving all that they carry to us? Are we missing the blessed good of either the sharpness or sweetness, the desired or the undesired? Are those secret doors of the spirit, hidden from all eyes like the stomata on the underside of the leaf, wide open, clean, free from the dust of earth?

O Breath of Life whose winds blow about me now, let me be all open to Thee today.

March 31

And the children of Reuben and the children of Gad called the altar Ed: *For, said they, it is a witness between us.*
Josh. 22:34 (RV)

When two people who love the Lord misunderstand each other and get into a tangle, there is generally a mistake which a few honest words will clear up.

Read Joshua 22. A long time ago two sets of people misunderstood each other. Both had made a mistake, the Reubenites and Gadites by not consulting anybody before building a great altar beside the Jordan, and the Israelites by putting a wrong interpretation on it.

But a few words straightened things out. The Reubenites, very much surprised that the Israelites could think anything so unkind and untrue, explained that they had acted "out of carefulness and of purpose." The Israelites accepted their explanation, and the matter ended with a word easy for us to remember, *Ed*. The thing which had almost caused a furious quarrel was turned to *Ed*, which meant that God (who is the God of Peace) was Witness.

If we have a misunderstanding with anyone, what about taking *Ed* as a little word of reminder to hurry up and make friends?

April 1

May the God who vouchsafes to you that same hope fill you
with all joy and peace through the exercise of your faith,
so that this hope of yours may be an overflowing fountain,
by the power of His Holy Spirit.
Rom. 15:13 (Way)

To understand the force of any Scripture, a good plan is to put it into opposite words. For example: "Now may the devil of discouragement fill you with all misery and disturbance in doubting, so that you may abound in distress, through the mighty working of the devil of discouragement."

Contrast that with the glorious truth of what Paul really wrote in Romans 15:13: *Now the God of Hope fill you with all joy and peace in believing, that ye may abound in hope, through the power of the Holy Ghost.*

Doesn't that make this hope of ours an overflowing fountain?

April 2

*All the day long did I spread out My hands unto a disobedi-
ent and gainsaying people.*
Rom. 10:21 (RV)

The metaphor is of a mother opening her arms to
call her child to her embrace. It has often helped me
when my faith and love burned low. If God could go on
doing such a loving thing "all day long" for years and
years, could not I go on loving and stretching out my
arms too? And so I learned to pray, "Love through me,
Love of God."

He is *the God of Patience and of Comfort* (Rom.
15:5) as well as *the God of Hope* (Rom. 15:13). Paul
must often have been discouraged and disappointed,
but deep in his heart these lovely names were spoken.
They can help us as they must have helped Paul.

❧

April 3

But let the righteous be glad; let them rejoice before God:
yea, let them exceedingly rejoice.
Ps. 68:3

In *Pilgrim's Progress* the Interpreter showed Christian the fire burning against the wall, and one standing by it, always casting much water upon it to quench it. But when he went to the "backside" of the wall, "he saw a man with a vessel of oil in his hand, of the which he did also continually cast, but secretly, into the fire."

There are times in most lives when it is hard to see how the fire is kept burning. We see him who casts the water. We do not see the Man with the vessel of oil in His hand. And yet He is there all the time. This "wall" which prevents us seeing what truly is, teaches us to walk by faith and not by sight.

But in His tender love our Lord does give us proof of His presence behind the wall. We cannot see Him, but we can hear Him speak. As a mother's voice can reassure her child in the dark, so indeed can His voice reassure us even though we cannot see Him.

"It may be my imagination." The whisper is as a drop of that water that is perpetually cast on the fire of faith and love. Let a question answer it for us. "Can imagination stay the heart? It may uplift it for a moment, but can it steady it, hold it in peace? Can it strengthen it?" No, it cannot, so let us trust and not be afraid. It was our Lord and not another who spoke to us.

Let us "be delighted with joy" then, as the Septuagint translates "exceedingly rejoice." Let us not waste one hour in fear, in dullness, in despondency, for He is never nearer than when we do not see Him but yet stay our hearts on Him.

April 4

Precious in the sight of the Lord is the death of His saints.
O Lord, truly I am Thy servant. . . . Thou hast loosed my
bonds. I will offer to Thee the sacrifice of thanksgiving.
Ps. 116:15–17

Sometimes even Christians write of death in a sad way. "We regret to announce," they say. The Salvation Army people are right in the way they put it: "Promoted to Glory."

Just after "Precious in the sight of the Lord" comes "Thou hast loosed my bonds." Think what a loosening that loosening is! No wonder the next words are, "I will offer to Thee the sacrifice of thanksgiving."

But those words first refer to the loosening of all bonds of sin. If anyone is conscious of any such bond, ask for it to be loosened now. Live as God's loosed ones.

≈

April 5

For this cause I obtained mercy, that in me first Jesus Christ might show forth all longsuffering, for a pattern to them which should hereafter believe on Him to life everlasting.
1 Tim. 1:16

Have you ever noticed the words, "His longsuffering for a pattern"? The longsuffering was for the difficult soul of Paul. So during those years when Paul was going his own way the Lord Jesus was noticing everything, feeling everything, suffering everything — always with one end in view. That longsuffering was "for a pattern" for us who also have to bear long with difficult souls.

April 6

And if any man say unto you, Why do ye this? say ye that the
Lord hath need of him; and straightway
he will send him hither.
Mark 11:3

Say ye… The Master saith, Where is the guest
chamber?…And he will show you a large
upper room furnished and prepared.
Mark 14:14–15

When our Lord Jesus comes again He will want to have a company of people upon whom He can count to do anything at a moment's notice, without fuss or demanding explanation. If that is to be so, we must prepare now. This means running off "at the double," obeying "on the dot," never stopping to argue or wonder why. How delightful it must have been for our Lord Jesus to be able to count on the owner of the colt and know that he would not disappoint Him. Wouldn't it be joy to give Him joy like that?

There was another unknown man in Jerusalem whom our Lord could trust to give what He wanted without any long explanation or preparation. He knew that it would be enough to say, *The Master saith, Where is the guestchamber?*

I think those two men whose names we do not know yet must be very glad now that they were ready at any minute to do anything for their Lord.

Are we like them in this readiness? Can we say what David's servants said to their king in 2 Samuel 15:15 (RV)? *Behold, thy servants are ready to do whatsoever my lord the king shall choose.*

April 7

Let all the people say, Amen. Praise ye the Lord.
Ps. 106:48

My friend wrote to me about two American missionaries who landed in England on their way to America. They had six children and they were very poor. Two of the children had typhoid and died. A third was so ill that her mother dared not leave her, even to see the other little ones laid in their graves. There were other difficulties and sorrowful circumstances, but in telling my friend of it all, that mother's face shone though it was wet with tears. She said: "It was all right. When God took full possession of me, He put an everlasting Amen to His will down in the bottom of my soul."

We are in the midst of much smaller troubles, but our perplexities can be very perplexing sometimes, and the devil tries to break in upon our peace. Let us ask our God to put *an everlasting Amen to His will* down in the bottom of our souls. *And let us ask Him to keep it there.*

April 8

I bow my knees unto the Father of our Lord Jesus Christ . . .
that He would grant you, according to the riches of His glory,
to be strengthened with might by His Spirit in the inner
man; that Christ may dwell in your hearts by faith; that ye,
being rooted and grounded in love, may be able . . . to know
the love of Christ, which passeth knowledge, that ye might be
filled with all the fullness of God.
Eph. 3:14–19:

The Holy Spirit is never an end in Himself. There is always a "that," a leading on to something beyond. Notice the three-times-repeated "that" in Ephesians 3:14–19.

The Spirit of God always leads on to the Christ of God. He strengthens with might in the inner man *that* Christ may dwell in our hearts by faith; *that* we being rooted and grounded in love may go on to comprehend that love; *that* as the empty shell on the shore is filled with the fullness of the sea as it washes up and over it, so we may be filled to the brim and to overflowing with the fullness of God. And God is Love.

So always we come back again to love. *Beloved, let us love* (1 John 4:7).

April 9

I will run the way of Thy commandments,
when Thou shalt enlarge my heart.
Ps. 119:32

Are you thinking something is impossible to do?
Perhaps you don't see why it should be done at all.

There are two possible reasons for this. One is a
kind of smallness of heart that the devil delights to encourage. The other is a dullness of sight that comes only
too easily if we look at ourselves and not "away unto"
our Lord Jesus.

The one certain way of escape from these two conditions is: Look at Calvary. Look till your dull eyes clear
and you see Love that poured forth all, counting nothing too precious to give for love of you. Don't hurry
away. Look, and as you look a change will pass over
you. You will see that what previously looked impossible is really the only possible thing for a follower of the
Crucified to do. It will be as if scales fell from your eyes
(as they did from Paul's), and you will see clearly again.

Then your narrow heart will become enlarged and
you will run to do what you could not even crawl towards doing before.

April 10

*O ye that love the Lord, see that ye hate
the thing which is evil.*
Ps. 97:10 (BCP)

Do we *hate* enough? I *hate all evil ways* the writer of
Psalm 119 said in verse 104, and in verse 128 *All false
ways I utterly abhor* (BCP).

Do we truly hate every false way? Or are we covering up something which will one day come out to our
shame before God and His holy angels? *There is nothing
covered, that shall not be revealed; and hid, that shall not
be known* (Matt. 10:26).

Do we hate unkind suspicions, whisperings, back-
bitings, all unlove?

Do we hate mushy friendships?

Do we hate all weakening things, or are we sliding
along in an easy kind of tolerance that is far removed
from the "hate" of such verses as this?

Do we hate laziness and slackness and all kinds of
selfishness?

See that you love all that God loves, but see that
you hate all that He hates. If we don't know how to
hate, we don't know how to love.

April 11

Draw out thy soul to the hungry.
Let thine own soul go out to the hungry (French).
Let the hungry ones find thy heart (German).
Lean thy soul to the hungry ones (Tamil).
Bestow on the hungry that which thy soul desireth
Isa. 58:10: (RV margin).

These are different ways of saying the same thing, but each adds something to it. The loving Lord strengthen us to live this life of love.

Don't forget, you who have to do with little children, that even a tiny child can be hungry though it doesn't quite know why. And bigger people can be hungry too, though they may not say so. Look out for the hungry and you will find them. He who has satisfied you with Himself will lead you to them.

April 12

*Then saith He unto them, My soul is exceeding sorrowful,
even unto death: tarry ye here, and watch with Me.
Matt. 26:38*

Mary Mozley of Central Africa wrote in a letter: "Somebody suggested this thought to me, and it came home to me the other day in reading about Christ in Gethsemane — that the way to show true sympathy is not to pity, but to stand by and strengthen the sufferer to do God's will. And in Gethsemane, when Christ turned to the three for sympathy, it was with the words, 'Watch with Me,' 'Stand by Me.' He asked for no pity, but for the strengthening which might *seem* a feeble help, just that they might let their presence and prayer tell there for Him, to strengthen Him to do the will of God."

The Lord help each one of us to "stand by" one another with just this kind of bracing sympathy.

April 13

For the Lord shall be thy confidence.
Prov. 3:26

When Gideon and his three hundred went out to face a foe far stronger than themselves they took a watchword, and they shouted it as they went forward. It was *The sword of the Lord, and of Gideon* (Judg. 7:18, 20).

Shall we take as our watchword now, *The Lord is our Confidence*? Shall we say it to our own hearts when they are tempted to fear, and to each other, and to those who question us, and to our Lord? Will you say it aloud to Him now, even as you read the words? *The Lord is our Confidence. Alleluia.*

❧

April 14

Ye shall not see Me henceforth, till ye shall say, Blessed is He
that cometh in the name of the Lord.
Matt. 23:39

The joyful entry into Jerusalem lay behind when our Lord spoke these words. He quoted from Psalm 118, which is a song of the Passion and the Glory which should follow. We have the rejection of our beloved Savior in this Psalm, and the triumph of evil, and then the glorious triumph of righteousness when He will be hailed as the Blessed One indeed.

Evil seems at present to be terrifically strong, and it seems to be triumphing everywhere. But it is on its way to its end. Good, not evil, will triumph. The gates of righteousness will open and the Righteous shall enter in. The Stone which the builders rejected will become the head stone of the corner, and His people shall say, *This is the Lord's doing; it is marvelous in our eyes. This is the day which the Lord hath made; we will rejoice and be glad in it* (Ps. 118:23–24).

But only those who have bound their sacrifice to the horns of the altar (v. 27) can be used to hasten the coming of that day.

Let us go afresh today unto the altar of God, unto God our exceeding joy (Ps. 43:4). Whatever our sacrifice may be (perhaps He only knows what it is) let us offer in His tabernacle that sacrifice of joy and sing. *Yea, I will sing praises unto the Lord.*

April 15

As for me, I will behold Thy face in righteousness:
I shall be satisfied, when I awake, with Thy likeness.
Ps. 17:15

A little Indian girl thought that if she wakened suddenly one morning she might see the angels as Jacob saw them.

Rotherham translates the last verse of Psalm 17, *I shall be satisfied when awakened by a vision of Thee,* or as the margin has it *by Thine appearing.*

It would be very joyful to be wakened by a vision of angels, by their appearing here in the room. But what will it be to be awakened by a vision of the Lord of the angels, our Lord whom we have loved so long and never seen? And then *We shall be like Him; for we shall see Him as He is* (1 John 3:2).

Perhaps we shall see the angels first, as I suppose the happy Lazarus did when he was "carried by angels" all the way home. But that will only be the beginning of joy. Revelation 22:3–4 tells us, *His servants shall serve Him: and they shall see His face; and His name shall be in their foreheads. That* will be heaven.

April 16

And wherefore have ye made us to come up out of Egypt, to
bring us in unto this evil place? it is no place of seed,
or of figs. . . .
Num. 20:5

"It is no place of figs," so the poor grumblers said.
They were continually grumbling, and generally about
food, which after all isn't the most important thing in
life. We have an expression, "I don't care a fig," meaning, "I don't care at all. It's not worth caring about." I
have been making a list of figs, those little things not
worth caring about and yet about which we are sometimes tempted to grumble. Perhaps you have a few private figs of your own — if so you can add them, pri-
vately, to the list.

I'm not in the place I want to be. I'm not doing the
work I want to do. I'm not with the particular friend
with whom I wanted to be. I don't feel very fit. I can't
help others much. (We forget that it doesn't matter that
we can't, if others can.) My plans are so often interrupted. I'm tired. I don't like this food. Somebody said
something about me. I have all sorts of temptations.
Nobody knows how hard it is for me. I can't help feeling downhearted. Figs, figs, figs — what will any one
of these things matter a hundred years hence, or ten, or
one? Then what do they matter now?

April 17

I can do all things through Christ which strengtheneth me.
Phil. 4:13

Now unto Him that is able to do exceeding abundantly
above all that we ask or think, according to the power that
worketh in us, unto Him be glory.
Eph. 3:20–21

When the Israelites were told not to gather manna on Saturday (their Sabbath), God made it possible for them to do without it by giving a double quantity on Friday (Exod. 16:22–26). If for any good reason we cannot gather our spiritual food on some particular day, God makes it all right. But this does not alter the ordinary rule of daily gathering our daily portion.

When, later on, God told the people that in the seventh year they were not to sow or even reap the grain that grew of itself, or gather the fruit that ripened on the undressed vines, it was a great test of faith (Lev. 25:1–5).

With the command came God's promise (Lev. 25:18–22) that He would give His special blessing in the sixth year, so that enough for three years would be gathered in that one year.

This is an illustration of what the Lord is always doing. He is continually asking us to do the impossible, and promising that He will make it possible. And as we obey, He does. Think of the things you thought quite impossible to face, but you *have* faced them — sometimes to your private astonishment, for you know that of yourself you couldn't.

We don't live on the natural plane. We are expected to count on the supernatural every time. Perhaps that was at the back of Paul's mind when he wrote, without an "if" or a "but" or a single reserve of any sort, *I can do all things through Christ which strengtheneth me.*

April 18

*Have this mind in you, which was also in Christ Jesus:
who...emptied Himself, taking the form of a servant.
Phil. 2:5, 7 (RV)*

*Forasmuch then as Christ suffered in the flesh, arm ye
yourselves also with the same mind.
1 Pet. 4:1 (RV)*

*Let this mind be in you, which was also in Christ
Jesus:* here the thought is selflessness. *Arm yourselves also
with the same mind:* here the thought is willingness for
suffering.

Do you seem unable to do much? Are you tempted
to feel you are of no use at all? The only thing that can
hinder a life from telling for Him is the mind that puts
self in the center, and the mind that refuses suffering.

Lord Jesus, give us the mind that was in Thee.

April 19

In all these things we are more than conquerors
through Him that loved us.
Rom. 8:37

These words are written of a general's duties, but the same duties are ours if we are given younger ones to help: "He should constantly impress on the minds of his officers and men the thought that the battle will not be lost because it must not be lost. Thus weakness is stayed, and all retreat cut off. The only open path leads forward to victory."

It is true for us all. *The only open path, the only path we must ever for one moment contemplate, leads forward to victory.*

Before a battle is lost on the field it is lost in the mind. If the Lord our Captain is in His rightful place there, we shall not think of defeat as among the possibilities of life.

God give us the soldier spirit, the spirit that thirsts to be more than conqueror.

April 20

He Himself knew what He would do.
John 6:6

It is interesting to compare the two miracles of feeding the multitude. In the feeding of the five thousand (John 6:5–13) the multitude was apparently part of a pilgrim caravan. The food was given soon, and help was not far off. It might have been found in the villages and the country round about.

The feeding of the four thousand was quite a different matter. The people were gathered from a Gentile region; they had continued for three days before they were fed; there was no help near. There was no question of finding help in villages. The place was a wilderness (Mark 8:1–9).

Westcott wrote: "Our situation, we think, is peculiarly difficult. Temptations are many and powerful. There is no quarter to which we can turn for immediate help. But let us not doubt. *The sense of our need is the condition of God's help. He will not remove our wants but He will satisfy them. He will not take away our temptations but He will give us strength to conquer them.*" Here and now in whatever is our wilderness, He will be our bread from heaven. He will satisfy our every need.

April 21

*If we walk in the light, as He is in the light, we have
fellowship one with another, and the blood of Jesus Christ
His Son cleanseth us from all sin. If we confess our sins, He is
faithful and just to forgive us our sins, and to cleanse us
from all unrighteousness.*
1 John 1:7, 9

Clement wrote: *"Let us gaze at the blood of Christ
and recognize how precious it is to His Father, because,
poured out for our salvation, it brought the grace of repentance to all the world."*

Do we ever fail to recognize how precious the blood
of His Son is to the Father? Do we ever ask lightly to be
forgiven, forgetting the cost of that forgiveness?

I remember as a small child seeing some fern seed-
lings belonging to a friend of my mother's, and I wanted
them very much. If I had asked for them they would
have been given to me, but I was too shy to ask. I said
to my little brother, "We might take them, and at night
we could confess and be forgiven."

I don't remember what we did, but my chief memory — and it has lasted all these years — is one of shame
for thinking such a thought. That kind of thought is the
very opposite of Clement's when he wrote those words
about the preciousness of the blood of Christ.

April 22

*I love the Lord, because He hath heard my voice
and my supplications.*
Ps. 116:1

As we look back on past years, they are full of memories of great sorrows and great joys also. If I were asked to give the sum of the years in a sentence I would write this: *I love the Lord, because He hath heard my voice and my supplications.* Never, never did He not hear. Never was He far away.

It will be the same with you. Just now you are in the midst of the pressure of life. One thing follows another so closely that you have hardly time to think, hardly time to realize how much you are being helped. But looking back it will be different. If there have been sorrows, you will see how marvelous His lovingkindness was. If there have been joys, it will be the same. If the time held just one steady round of service it will still be the same. Every day, every hour will seem to you then as if these words were written across it: *I love the Lord because He hath heard.*

So love Him now, rejoice in Him now, however things are, for it is true today — He hears your voice and your supplications.

April 23

And with them Heman and Jeduthun, and the rest that were chosen, who were expressed by name, to give thanks to the Lord, because His mercy endureth for ever.
1 Chron. 16:41

In 1 Chronicles 16 various names are mentioned, and then suddenly in verse 41 come the words, *And the rest that were chosen, who were expressed by name.* It is as if God said: "I have another roll book and each one of you, My servants, has been chosen and expressed by name in that book of Mine."

We all like secrets — happy secrets. Here is one of God's happy secrets. In His roll book, not published on earth but eternal in the heavens, we, even we, are expressed by name.

What is your work today? Think of it, you were chosen for just that work, and you are expressed by name in the roll book of your God. Even if you are ill and unable to work, you can do what God's unnamed servants of old did: they were chosen *to give thanks to the Lord,* and so are you.

So don't let us slacken, but fight the good fight and run the good race even unto the end.

April 24

My work is for a King.
Ps. 45:1 (RV margin)

What is your work? To help sick people, or little people, or tiresome people? To cook and clean, to make and mend, to work in office or shop or factory? To do the hundreds of odds and ends that every day brings?

Does the whisper ever come to you, "What is the use?" If it does, let these words answer it. *My work is for a King.*

> For the quiet joy of Duty,
> Praise, praise I sing,
>> For the commonplace and lowly,
>> Set with pleasure high and holy,
>> In each unromantic thing,
>> Praise, praise to Thee, my King.

❧

April 25

And one ran and filled a sponge full of vinegar, and put it
on a reed, and gave Him to drink.
Mark 15:36

When we read, in Matthew, Mark and John, of how a soldier ran and filled a sponge with the only drink that was near at hand, and offered it to our Lord Jesus, don't we all feel how good it must have been to be that soldier, or even that sponge? For if there had not been a sponge to soak up the vinegar, the soldier could not have met this last human need of our dear Lord.

That sponge was once a living thing. It had to die before it could be empty. A sponge is only the skeleton of a creature or of many creatures.

This is one of the figures of the true which are everywhere waiting to speak to us. It seems to say: "There must be death to that which perhaps is very life to you, before you can be empty enough to be filled to quench the thirst of the Savior of the world." "There is no life except by death," nor is there any service of the sort that satisfies His heart.

Self must die — that is the message of the sponge.

April 26

*The merciful and gracious Lord hath so done His marvelous
works: that they ought to be had in remembrance.*
Ps. 111:4 (BCP)

For the Love that like a screen
Sheltered from the might-have-been,
Be Thy Name adored.

Do you ever thank God for His daily preservations?
For every time the car goes out and returns in safety?
For His gift, guarded so wonderfully, of sight, hearing,
speech, feeling, power to walk and run and work, and
to enjoy life?

Don't wait till "something happens" that we must
pray about, but praise for every day that "nothing happens." And when there is some very special lovingkindness, remember the great word, *The merciful and gracious Lord hath so done His marvelous works: that they
ought to be had in remembrance.*

April 27

And behold, there talked with Him two men, which were Moses and Elijah; who appeared in glory, and spake of His decease which He was about to accomplish at Jerusalem. And it came to pass, as they were parting, Peter said unto Jesus, Master, it is good for us to be here.
Luke 9:30–31, 33 (RV)

Have you ever found yourself making a great deal of a small trouble? I have. Especially goodbyes. But what of the goodbye of this story?

Elijah and Moses had been talking with our Lord Jesus of the agonizing death which He had so soon to "accomplish." They must have felt it far more acutely than we can imagine. What must that minute of parting have been to them and to Him? Think what it would be to say goodbye to someone you loved, who had to go through an awful operation without anesthetic — but that gives one only the faintest idea of what it was to those two men to leave our Lord that day.

But we read of no fuss. They went away so quietly that *as they were parting* Peter could speak to our Lord, just as if He and they were not even then going through this tremendous goodbye.

It makes us feel ashamed of ever making much of any trouble. The heavenly people don't. Our Lord never did.

April 28

I cried unto the Lord with my voice, and
He heard me out of His holy hill.
Ps. 3:4

"Feet accustomed to the road to God can find it in the dark," wrote Dr. Maclaren on Psalm 3:4. Our work is to teach others how to find "the road to God," and how to know it so well that they will be able to "find it in the dark." Could there be a happier work than this?

Scholars tell us that the tenses of verse 4 express a habitual act and a constant result. *I cried . . . He heard me.* Is it not wonderful to know that it is always so? It is as if our Father had no one in all the world to care for but you, but me, but the one we are trying to help.

Truly His love passes knowledge!

April 29

*Into Thine hand I commit my spirit: Thou hast
redeemed me, O Lord God of truth.*
Ps. 31:5

Do you ever find prayer difficult because of tired-
ness or dryness? When that is so, it is an immense help
to let the Psalms and hymns we know by heart say
themselves or sing themselves inside us. This is possible
anywhere and at any time.

We can't be mistaken in using this easy, open way
of prayer, for our Lord Jesus used it. His very last prayer,
when He was far too tired to pray as He usually did, was
Psalm 31:5. Every Jewish mother used to teach her child
to say those words as a good-night prayer.

Hymns, little prayer-songs of our own, even the
simplest of them, can sing us into His love. Or more
truly, into the consciousness of His love, for we are never for one moment out of it.

April 30

*That none of you might be unnerved by your present trials:
for you yourselves know that they are our appointed lot.*
1 Thess. 3:3 (Weymouth)

Have you difficulties? *They are our appointed lot.*
Have you trials? *They are our appointed lot.*

Those five words were written to people who might
any day find themselves in prison, tortured, lonely, oppressed. Here if we have to have a tooth out, we have an
injection. There was no injection for the Christians of
Thessalonica. Let us not forget that when we are tempted to fuss over trifles, and call things trials which are
mere nothings.

Still, there *are* trials sometimes, and they may look
very big. But *they are our appointed lot* — we were never
promised ease. The early Christians were not taught to
expect it. Don't let us slip into the expectation of the
easy. It isn't our appointed lot.

But for us there is always another word (2 Cor.
12:9): *My grace is sufficient for thee.*

May 1

*They did take their food with gladness and singleness
of heart, praising God.*
Acts 2:46 (RV)

Why do people think it is a dull thing to be a
Christian? Even our meal times should be happy.
The early disciples took their meals with great happiness, and the Lord took notice of these happy meals and
even thought it worth recording for us to read.

May "the delightfulness of the Lord our God be
upon" us all, at meal times and all times today (Ps.
90:17 Rotherham).

❧

May 2

I die daily. 1 Cor. 15:31

That which cometh upon me daily, the care of all the churches. 2 Cor. 11:28

"The Beloved clothed Himself in the garments of His lover that he might be His companion in glory for ever. So the lover desired to wear crimson garments daily, that his dress might be like that of his Beloved" (Ramon Lull).

Sometimes we are tempted to be surprised, as though some strange things happened unto us, because of the "crimson garment daily." For some there is the care that comes daily, the care about the souls of others. This is part of the fellowship of His sufferings. For some there is the daily assault of temptation, the suffering of being tempted. "Why cannot there be a little respite? If there is not one thing there is always another." That is how we feel and it is true. It always has been true. *I die daily.*

To Ramon Lull, who lived more than 600 years ago, crimson meant suffering. He did not ask that he might wear the crimson garment sometimes, but always. He wanted to be willing to die daily, "that his dress might be like that of his Beloved."

He worked among the Muslims of North Africa, was banished, returned and was stoned to death.

❧

May 3

Greater is He that is in you, than he that is in the world.
1 John 4:4

Sometimes we are tempted to feel, "I want to serve God wholly and to live for others, but Satan's power is very great. How can I withstand him to the end? Even our Lord Jesus called him the prince of this world (John 12:31). He is too strong for me."

There are two Greek words which are translated "prince" in our New Testament. One is *archon,* a ruler, the common word used for the rulers of the people. This is the word our Lord uses in speaking of Satan. The other word is *Archegos,* which means a founder, author, file-leader, true and ultimate Prince. This is used for our Lord Jesus Christ.

Satan is only the prince; he is mighty but not Almighty, *archon* not *Archegos. Greater is He that is in you than he who is in the world.* He is the Prince. Trust your Prince.

May 4

Hast thou not called Me as it were a home?
Jer. 3:4 (Septuagint)

Home is one of our very dearest words, because all that we know of human love is wrapped up in it. I have been applying this word, which comes only in the Septuagint, to our Sunday morning worship. *Hast thou not called Me as it were a home?*

It is true that we are always there, at home with Him, but our time of worship is meant to be a specially joyful coming home together — a little lovely foretaste of what will be by and by, when we see Him face to face.

As we return from the "journey" of the week, let us believe in the welcome that awaits us, and eagerly and joyfully hasten to our home.

May 5

Then the king commanded Ebed-melech the Ethiopian,
saying, Take from hence thirty men with thee, and take
up Jeremiah the prophet out of the dungeon, before he die.
. . . And Ebed-melech the Ethiopian said unto Jeremiah,
Put now these old cast clouts and rotten rags under thine
armholes under the cords. And Jeremiah did so.
Jer. 38:10–12

The dungeon where Jeremiah was kept was one of those horrible pits that were used in olden times as prisons. The king only told Ebed-melech to take thirty men and pull Jeremiah out of the dungeon with ropes, before he died. But that kind man, whose name means "Servant of the King," took the trouble to go and fetch pieces of cast-off clothes and old soft rags. He told Jeremiah to put them under his armpits to keep the ropes from hurting him as they pulled him out.

In Matthew 25:40 we read what the King of Kings must have said to Servant of the King, Ebed-melech. *Inasmuch as ye have done it unto one of the least of these My brethren, ye have done it unto Me.*

Think of it, every little thoughtful kindness we do for someone in need, our Lord notices. He takes it as service done to Him. Let us serve Him by serving others, however humbly, today.

May 6

He is altogether lovely. This is my Beloved, and this is my
Friend, O daughters of Jerusalem.
Song of Sol. 5:16

"The lover went through a city, and asked if there were none with whom he might speak of his Beloved as he wished. And they showed him a poor man who was weeping for love, and who sought a companion with whom to speak of love" (Ramon Lull).

Sometimes there is a poor man quite near us and we do not recognize him. He may be in disguise. He may not seem poor, or as though he had tears in his heart, and yet he may be longing for just what we are longing to give. Often a shyness, a reserve, some veil of our own weaving comes down between us, and we speak of the work of our Beloved but never of Him Himself.

Let us ask that our eyes may be opened to see the poor man in the city. He may be a little child, a difficult person, a fellow-worker, a guest, a stranger who drifts across our path perhaps only once. He may be a friend whom we could reach by a letter.

A little while ago, one who had only just come to know the Lord said, "Isn't He *delightful?*" She spoke of Him; do we?

May 7

So teach us to number our days, that we may
apply our hearts unto wisdom.
Ps. 90:12

Some while ago I was given two big pieces of soap, and I use both every day. For a good while I saw very little difference in either, but gradually I saw that both were just a little less. Of course one can't at the same time both give and keep, and soap is always giving. Every time you use it, it gives you something of itself, so naturally it becomes less and less.

Did you ever think of life as a piece of soap? Every day, hour, minute, it is giving you something of itself. Soon it will have given all, and then there won't be any more of it here. When we are young we think things will go on just as they are forever. But they don't.

Next time you use your soap, will you think of David's prayer in Psalm 90:12?

May 8

*Not that I have already obtained, or am already made
perfect: but I press on, if so be that I may apprehend that for
which also I was apprehended by Christ Jesus.*
Phil. 3:12 (RV)

We live too hurried lives, sometimes; talk too
much; think too little. *With the goal in view am I racing
on* is Way's version of verse 14.

I am pressing on — that was Paul's word. Is it ours?
For what has our Lord laid hold of us? Are we laying
hold of that? Or are we content to live the ordinary life?

Let us *press on* today through all hindering things,
distracting thoughts, unworthy feelings. Let us press on
through all feelings of sloth or discouragement or fear,
to the place where our God can speak to us in the stillness, and hold us close to His heart.

❧

May 9

And they took two princes of the Midianites, Oreb and
Zeeb; and they slew Oreb upon the rock Oreb,
and Zeeb they slew at the winepress of Zeeb.
Judg. 7:25

Oreb and Zeeb were two enemies of the Lord. Oreb means Raven, and Zeeb means Wolf. Our nearest bird to the raven is the crow, and we know how it behaves. It hops up sideways, looking as if it isn't thinking of anything much, and then suddenly snatches some trifle we have forgotten to take care of, and flies off with it. And we know something of a wolf's habits. It is not very nice for the one whom he carries off to his den.

Sometimes temptation comes to us like a crow, in a casual kind of way. Before we know it, something we should have been careful of just disappears — good temper, good manners, thoughtfulness for one another, something that perhaps seems a little thing and yet really isn't.

Sometimes temptation comes like a wolf, and rushes upon us. Then something dreadful happens; a lie is told, a dishonest thing is done, and unless we awaken to our danger we are soon in the wolf's den.

But just as the Raven was conquered and slain on a rock called the Raven, and the Wolf at a place called the Wolf, so in the very heart where that temptation is most at home (so that people say, "Oh, she is such a cross person! Oh, he is such an untruthful person!"), there, just *there*, will be victory. Only we must obey the directions given to all who are tempted. They are written in Ephesians 6:16–18.

May 10

*We remember the fish, which we did eat in Egypt freely; the
cucumbers, and the melons, and the leeks,
and the onions, and the garlick.*
Num. 11:5

I should fulfill Thy will, O my God: I am content to do it.
Ps. 40:10 (BCP):

To think of nice things one can't have is to become
discontented and grumpy. Is there something you want
and can't have today? Are you tempted to grouse about
it? Repeat that little string of six words to yourself quite
slowly and solemnly: "Fish, cucumbers, melons, leeks,
onions, garlic." If you haven't time for all six just say
"Cucumbers," and see what will happen. First you will
laugh. Then in a flash you will remember those foolish
and ungrateful people whose story you know so well.
You will remember, too, how patiently God bore with
them; and you will be ashamed that even for one moment you joined forces with them.

We are all sure to be tempted by thoughts of fish,
cucumbers, melons, onions, leeks and garlic — things
we would like, but cannot have at present. But there is
another set of six words which is as happy as the first set
of six is unhappy. They were spoken by our Lord Jesus
Christ about His Father's will: *I am content to do it.*

Which set of six will you take for your own? You
can't have both; they won't mix. So choose.

May 11

Then said Martha unto Jesus, Lord, if Thou hadst been here, my brother had not died. But I know, that even now, whatsoever Thou wilt ask of God, God will give it Thee.
John 11:21–22

Martha said, "But I know that even now. . . ." Westcott's note on this is, *"Faith reaches forth to that which it does not grasp."* "Even now" — the utter abandon of faith that accepts what it has not received.

This is triumphant faith. It is so easy to have faith for what we have good reason to hope for. It is not so easy when we do not receive what we expected.

But we have our Lord's own "Even so" to help us (Matt. 11:26): *Even so, Father: for so it seemed good in Thy sight.* It is the "Yes, Father," of the unoffended, the "Even so, Father" which accepts all mysteries.

Lord, evermore give us *this* faith.

May 12

Let us run with patience the race that is set before us.
Heb. 12:1

He hath said, I will never leave thee, nor forsake thee. So
that we may boldly say, The Lord is my Helper,
and I will not fear.
Heb. 13:5–6

Watching an obstacle race made me think of the
race we are called to run. While we are in the middle of
loops and tires and ladders and sacks we may be tempted to forget that they did not put themselves there.
They are there on purpose. What would be the point of
an obstacle race if there were no obstacles? It would be
foolish to say, "Couldn't you clear these obstacles off the
field, and make the race nice and easy?"

And yet that is exactly what we often ask God to do
for us. "Please make it a bit easier, it's too hard for me."
That is a poor sort of prayer, and there is not a single
promise in the Bible which we can take and spread before our Father and say, "See, my Father, You promised to make the race easy." So it cannot be the kind of
prayer He likes His runners to bring to Him.

There are many promises that we can bring. Here is
one. It was written in a letter to people who were running in an obstacle race, and the obstacles were simply
tremendous. The author wrote about being properly
prepared for the race, and about running with patience.

He wanted to give them a strong word of comfort too, so he wrote: "God has said, I will never leave you nor forsake you. So you may boldly say, The Lord is my Helper, I will not fear."

Next time we feel like giving up as we jump our bars, or scramble up our ladders, or dive through our rings, or struggle through our old tires, or stagger along in our sacks, let us listen and we shall hear that word, "I will never leave you nor forsake you."

❧

May 13

Casting all your care upon Him; for He careth for you.
1 Pet. 5:7

An old woman was walking along the road very wearily, carrying a big bundle, and a friendly carter gave her a lift. Presently he turned round and saw that she was still holding her bundle in her arms, instead of putting it down in the cart. When he asked her why she did so foolish a thing, she replied: "It is asking too much of you, to carry my bundle as well as me."

You know and laugh at that story, but did you ever do just the same yourself? Are you a little bit anxious about the test of the difficult? Do you ever wonder how you are going to win through?

Next time that thought comes, remember the old woman and her bundle. He who carries you, carries your bundle too. *Casting all your care upon Him; for He careth for you,* does not mean "Cast all your other burdens, but be sure to carry this particular one yourself." All means all.

May 14

And He led them on safely, so that they feared not.
Ps. 78:53

So He ... guided them by the skillfulness of His hands.
Ps. 78:72

"And He guided them with hope" is the Septuagint reading. The God of Hope guided with hope. "And guided them by the skillfulness of His hands"; Rotherham translates it "the discernment." He adds a note: "A beautiful expression. How much all manual workers need to put their discernment into their hands."

He will lead us on safely through the working hours of this new day with its new experiences of discipline and perhaps sorrow and disappointment. There will be experiences of joy, too, for we follow the Lord of Joy. He will not lose hope about us. He will guide us with hope, and with the discernment of His hands.

So there is no room for fear.

❧

May 15

I counsel thee to buy of Me gold tried in the fire,
that thou mayest be rich.
Rev. 3:18

Pure gold, like unto clear glass.
Rev. 21:18

When God, the Creator of metals, chooses a metal to signify something He wants us to possess, His thought includes all which that metal is.

"Of all metals gold is the most malleable and ductile. It can be beaten into plates of leaves so thin that it takes 300,000 of them placed one above another to make one inch, and the gold then is transparent enough to allow rays of light to pass through."

The word *malleable* comes from the Latin and means a metal that can be hammered out. *Ductile* is also from the Latin and means capable of being drawn out into wire; the dictionary gives "tough, tractable, docile" among its meanings.

It is only beaten gold that is like unto clear glass. The hammer has fallen on that gold till there is nothing left but a golden transparency. *I counsel thee to buy of Me gold tried in the fire — pure gold, like unto clear glass.* The fire comes first, then the hammer. Is the price to be paid to buy such gold a willingness for the fire and the hammer?

And ductile, leadable. An Indian goldsmith can

draw out a piece of gold in wires as fine as a hair. That quality which Paul calls *the meekness and gentleness of Christ* (2 Cor. 10:1) is not naturally in us. We are not "tough" yet "tractable" and "docile." *I counsel thee to buy of Me.*

❧

May 16

*The Lord is my Rock, and my Fortress, and my Deliverer;
my God, my strength, in whom I will trust.*
Ps. 18:2

*For the mountains shall depart, and the hills be removed;
but My kindness shall not depart from thee,
neither shall the covenant of My peace be removed,
saith the Lord that hath mercy on thee.*
Isa. 54:10

The mountains shall depart, and the hills be removed;
sometimes we forget that we have been told it will be so.
*BUT My kindness shall not depart from thee, neither shall
the covenant of My peace be removed, saith the Lord that
hath mercy on thee* (Isa. 54:10).

Has His kindness ever departed from us? Has the
covenant of His peace been broken? No, never for an
hour. Solomon said, *There hath not failed one word of all
His good promise* (1 Kings 8:56). We can say it too. *Not
one thing hath failed* of all the good things which He
spake concerning us; all are come to pass unto us, and
not one thing hath failed thereof (Josh. 23:14).

Is it not then sheer treason to fear anything of any
sort? "Nothing can come wrong to my Lord in His
sweet working." He takes away our mountains and hills,
on whose strength we relied, so that He may the more
become the Rock of our heart and our Fortress forever.

May 17

A Song of Pause.
Ps. 9:16 (Septuagint)

The Lord has heard the desire of the poor: Thine ear has
inclined to the preparation of their heart.
Ps. 10:17 (Septuagint)

Higgaion Selah. Does that mean anything to you?
In the Septuagint it is *A Song of Pause.* In some versions
the translation is *meditation,* and in others *resounding
music.* It seems something like our Dawn Chorus, when
the birds burst into song and then are still, and then fall
to singing again. That lovely hour is a Song of Pause.

Could there be a lovelier name for our morning
quiet time with our Lord? A time of worship and adoration which is stillness, meditation, resounding music,
listening and prayer? There could be no lovelier name,
either, for the whole day, if only we learned to keep it as
a Song of Pause.

Don't rush into God's presence as though it were a
common thing. We have a God who notices the preparation of the heart. Micah 6:8 tells us to walk *humbly*
with our God, and then we have His promise that He
Himself will prepare our heart. *Lord, Thou hast heard the
desire of the humble: Thou wilt prepare their heart, Thou
wilt cause Thine ear to hear.*

❧

May 18

He hath left off to be wise, and to do good.
Ps. 36:3

The Septuagint says, *He is not inclined to understand how to do good.* That is one of the signs of what God calls wickedness. He does not treat it lightly, and to act as though He would is dangerous. It is taking advantage of His patience. It is to flatter yourself in your own eyes (see verse 2), and that is a deadly thing to do. God has set a terrible *until* to that: *For he flattereth himself in his own eyes, until his iniquity be found to be hateful.*

In Psalm 32 David tells of what life was to him all the time he covered his sin and went on as usual, hoping that God did not notice it. The Septuagint of verse 4 says, *I became thoroughly miserable while a thorn was fastened in me.*

Are you thoroughly miserable? Then that means that His hand is heavy upon you. But if you have yielded to the pressure of God's heavy hand upon the thorn within, then take comfort, because with Him is pardon.

But do not hasten away from His cross. Think of the hands that were pierced with iron thorns because of that thorn in you; think of the pierced feet; think of the crown of thorns. Have not your hands sinned? Have not your feet walked in sinful ways? What have the thoughts you have thought been?

Do not hurry past these questions. Do not think it is enough to say to the One whom you have wronged, "Please forgive me," and forget what His forgiveness cost. There is far too little sense of sin among us, too little "thorough misery," too easy a repentance.

⌇

May 19

But when he saw the wind boisterous, he was afraid; and
beginning to sink, he cried, saying, Lord, save me. And
immediately Jesus stretched forth His hand, and caught him.
Matt. 14:30–31

"And *beginning* to sink." Only four words, but they
bring us the certainty that we will never sink, for Peter
never sank. It is like that word in Psalm 94:18, *When I*
said, My foot slippeth — yes, in that very moment — *Thy*
mercy, O Lord, held me up.

Sometimes a single word may make all the difference to us, lifting us up, strengthening and refreshing
us. Let us be careful not to miss these words of life,
which come so suddenly, perhaps in the midst of the
day's work.

Samuel Rutherford wrote: "In your temptations,
run to the promises: they may be our Lord's branches hanging over the water, that our Lord's silly, half-
drowned children may take a grip of them." And those
boughs never break.

❧

May 20

For I, saith the Lord, will be unto her a wall of fire round
about, and will be the glory in the midst of her.
Zech. 2:5

One night I was greatly tempted because I felt so helpless. There was nothing I could do to protect you, and the burden was heavy. Suddenly it was as if a voice said, "Leave it to Me, child, leave it to Me."

Near me were two pure white lilies, which had opened after the last thunderstorm. Perhaps it was they which gave the last line in this song:

Leave it to Me, child, leave it to Me,
Dearer thy garden to Me than to thee.
Lift up thy heart, child, lift up thine eyes,
Nought can defeat Me, and nought can surprise.

Leave it to Me, child, leave it to Me,
Trust in the wall of fire, look up and see
Stars in their courses shine through the night.
Both are alike to Me — darkness and light.

Leave it to Me, child, leave it to Me.
Let slip the burden too heavy for thee.
That which I will, My Hand shall perform,
Fair are the lilies that weather the storm.

May 21

O Lord, by these things men live, and in all these things
is the life of my spirit.
Isa. 38:16

O Lord, I am oppressed; undertake for me
[margin: ease me].
Isa. 38:14

Hezekiah's story comes in 2 Kings 18–20 and Isaiah 38.

There had been close walk with God and he prospered wherever he went. He fought the Lord's battles and saw His victories. It is one long tale of triumphant life, the kind of life that is full of light and certainty, in spite of Satanic opposition. There were quick answers to prayer, *That which thou hast prayed to Me . . . I have heard* (2 Kings 19:20).

We know the sunlit joy of such days. They may be full of battle but they are the very kind the heart most desires and most delights in.

Then suddenly the path he has been following leads down a long slope to the levels of life. He misses the exhilaration of the peaks, and his heart longs for what used to be. He cries, *O Lord, I am oppressed; undertake for me — ease me. O Lord, by these things men live, and in all these things is the life of my spirit.* Not only the hours of exultation when we walk under opened heaven and we *see,* but also those hours when we do not see, or hear, or feel, and only cry, "Lord, ease me" — by these things men live. And in all these things are the life of the spirit, life that holds in it the seed of life for others.

❧

May 22

That which . . . our hands have handled,
of the Word of life.
1 John 1:1

Handle Me, and see.
Luke 24:39

That handling is not for us today, but even so the word shows something that belongs to us all.

We sing, "When I survey the wondrous cross." How much do we "survey"? How real is it to us? Those wounds, how much do they truly mean to us?

If only once and for one moment a deep insight were given us, and we saw and our hands "handled" these sacred things, everything in life would fall into its right place. We would never make our molehills into mountains. All that is appointed for us would seem as nothing in comparison with that which our hands had handled of the Word of Life, who for our sake was made suffering human flesh. We would live in the spirit of an old prayer, "Let there be no exaggeration of the way I go today."

❧

May 23

We know not what we should pray for as we ought.
Rom. 8:26

We know that all things work together for good
to them that love God.
Rom. 8:28

How true it is, we do not know what we should pray for. "But we do know that all things work together for good." Darby emphasizes that "we *do* know" and says it looks back to "we do *not* know."

Another light on that familiar word, Romans 8:28, comes through Rotherham's rendering: "God causeth all things to work together for good."

What does it matter what we do not know, when we do know this?

"And sure am I, that, on those who love God, all things are with one purpose working to bring blessings — yes, on those to whom, according to His providential plan, He has cried 'Come ye to Me!'" (Way).

May 24

The fear of the Lord tendeth to life.
Prov. 19:23

If the fear of the Lord (the reverence of the Lord) tends to life, then anything irreverent tends to death. It is to death that the devil is continually seeking to lure us.

How can we prepare ourselves so that we may be usable to the utmost, either to speak for our Lord or to pray? One certain way lies along the line of reverence. A test question is: "What is our attitude when we are shown something wrong in ourselves?" If someone else has pointed it out, is our first reaction, "Who told him? Do others know? What do they think?" If self-pity and self-justification are our response, or if we sit down in depression, then we have missed something. The reverence of the Lord is not in us. Calvary is not the tremendous thing that matters most to us. Our "I" has risen up. We do not see our sins as the nails that pierced our Savior's hands and feet. We do not feel ourselves to be the hammer driving in again those torturing nails.

Let us take off our shoes from off our feet in His burning presence that He may search and purge us, and prepare us for His service.

May 25

And Enoch walked with God.
Gen. 5:22

The Lord appeared to Abram, and said unto him, I am the
Almighty God [El Shaddai]; walk before Me.
Gen. 17:1

Walk with God; walk before God; walk in fellowship with God. It is that ordinary every day walk which will be attacked. And yet we need never crash. We have two glorious words with which to confront the adversary: *But God.*

We are all weakness, *But God is the strength of my heart* (Ps. 73:26).

Before the command was given to Abram he was told that wonderful name of the Lord. *I am El Shaddai,* the Almighty God, the God who is enough. He is our eternal strength, and with Him we can walk this day and every day of our lives.

May 26

And it came to pass, that, while they communed together and reasoned, Jesus Himself drew near, and went with them.
Luke 24:15

Rotherham translates it: "Jesus Himself drawing near was journeying with them." How good and comforting it is to know that the fact of His Presence did not depend on their feeling Him near. He was near; He was journeying with them.

If even for an hour that blessed Presence seems far distant, and we are (as they were) cast down and in trouble, the quickest way to recover is to do what Rotherham says they did. "They came to a stand" (v. 17).

There was a pause for quietness, then questions and time given for answers; and then *Abide with us* (v. 29).

As He sat at meat with them, He took bread, and blessed it, and brake, and gave to them. And their eyes were opened, and they knew Him (Luke 24:30–31).

❧

May 27

*It is God which worketh in you both to will
and to do of His good pleasure.*
Phil. 2:13

Jacob Boehme, who was born in 1575, wrote, "Hold Thou Thy Grace in love in Jesus Christ over me, and give me a happy spirit in which to work Thy wonders. Let Thy holy angel rule me all my life long, and be in me my willing, my working, and my fulfilling."

There are times when we get to the end of our own willing. What utter rest and joy it is, then, to count upon this word in Philippians 2:13, and to pray as Jacob Boehme did so long ago, *Be in me my willing, my working and my fulfilling.*

May 28

So, as much as in me is, I am ready to preach the gospel
to you that are at Rome also.
Rom. 1:15

Paul wrote this before he knew what it would cost
him to go to Rome via Jerusalem. But he knew he was
ready.

It was different with the people who loved him.
"Take care of yourself," they said in effect. To that he
had only one answer, Acts 21:13, *What mean ye to weep*
and to break mine heart? for I am ready not to be bound
only, but also to die at Jerusalem for the name of the Lord
Jesus.

As we go deeper into the fellowship of His sufferings we need a deeper prayer for each other. We must
be ready, not only to suffer ourselves, but to allow those
we love to have the privilege of suffering too. Moule understands Philippians 1:29 to mean: "To you there has
been granted as an actual boon — for the sake of Christ
not only the believing on Him but also the suffering for
His sake; a sacred privilege when it is involved by loyalty
to such a Master!"

Let us be ready to accept that privilege, not only for
ourselves but also, which is harder, for others.

Purge from the earthly, give us love divine,
Father, like Thine, like Thine.

❧

May 29

In my flesh shall I see God: whom I shall see for myself, and
mine eyes shall behold, and not another.
Job 19:26–27

I shall see God for myself, *and not another; not a*
stranger is the KJV margin. I shall not have to learn to
know and love Him, for it will be the God who has led
me all my life long — and not another.

No stranger's face will meet us on the day we die.
We shall be awakened by the vision of His face — only
His.

A little girl was slowly dying in her home in India.
A Christian doctor who was called to see her told her of
our Lord Jesus. After a little while she began to understand and love Him. One day she said: "I don't know
anyone in heaven. I shall feel very shy there."

"But you know our Lord Jesus," said the doctor.
"You won't be shy with Him." She was comforted. Soon
after that she saw Him — not another, not a stranger,
but the Lord who loved her and gave Himself for her.

❧

May 30

My brethren, count it all joy when ye fall into divers temptations; knowing this, that the trying of your faith worketh patience. But let patience have her perfect work, that ye may be perfect and entire, wanting nothing.
Jas. 1:2–4

Patience may seem rather a dull virtue — like meekness, which we can mistake for weakness. But Rotherham, Moffatt, Weymouth and Darby translate patience as "endurance," which is one of the challenging words of the world. And James suggests that if only we welcome the chance to learn to endure there will, one day, be a perfecting and the disciple shall be as his Master.

Does that sound too wonderful to be true? We have sure words about it (Luke 6:40 RV): *every one when he is perfected shall be as his master.*

Life that is life indeed does not go under when assaulted, but rises to meet the trial of its faith, "and greets it as pure joy," as Moffatt puts it. Does it seem impossible? Let other verses help us. *Not that I have already obtained, or am already made perfect: but I press on. I can do all things* (even this) *in Him that strengtheneth me* (Phil. 3:12; 4:13 RV).

So let us run with patience the race that is set before us, looking unto Jesus (turning our eyes away from all else), *Who holdeth our soul in life: and suffereth not our feet to slip* (Ps. 66:8 BCP).

May 31

Continuing instant [to persevere toward] in prayer.
Rom. 12:12

Ask, and ye shall receive.
John 16:24

Why need there be a continuing in prayer? Our Father needs no reminder. I do not think that anywhere He explains this matter to us, but this thought of "persevering" runs through the Old Testament, and the new Testament is full of it too.

Westcott's note on John 16:24 is: *"Ask:* the command implies a continuous prayer, and not a single petition."

It is like our Father to tell us to do what our human hearts urge us to do: go on asking. It is like that other word (James 5:13), "Is any merry? let him sing." The very frogs want to sing when they are merry, and so do we.

But the command to continue in prayer is not an easy thing. It can mean conflict, wrestling, agony. Forces are moving in the unseen about us, and prayer influences those movements. In Exodus 17:11 we read that when Moses held up his hand Israel prevailed, and when he let down his hand Amalek prevailed. It is a law of the spiritual world, not explained, just stated.

Lord, help us to continue, to persevere in prayer. Hold our hands steady until the going down of the sun (Exod. 17:12).

June 1

*God spake unto him [Moses], saying, I am the God of
Abraham, and the God of Isaac, and the God of Jacob. He is
not the God of the dead, but the God of the living.*
Mark 12:26–27

*Therefore let us, like them — since we have encompassing us
that vast cloud of witnesses for the truth — put aside every
encumbrance, put off the garment of sin that can so readily
trammel our efforts, and with strong endurance let us race
along the course that stretches before us, turning our eyes
away from all else toward Jesus.*
Heb. 12:1–2 (Way)

Our Lord Jesus has taught us to call the dead, the
living. When a match is played or races are run,
a crowd gathers round to watch. Round about us now,
like a dense but shining cloud, a great company has
gathered to watch us playing the game of life and running the race. What would it be if suddenly we could
see that which is truly all about us, the living ones of
the unseen world? We cannot, but we are not meant to
forget them. They do not forget us. There will be unseen
"witnesses" all around us today, praising God for what
He is doing for us as with strong endurance we race
along the course set for today.

June 2

Exceeding great and precious promises.
2 Pet. 1:4

"Promises precious and supreme"; "precious and wondrous"; "precious and very great." To read the different translations is like turning a jewel in the light. Each turn shows some new beauty.

In the end we shall find every promise perfectly fulfilled. Then why should we not let our hearts rest in peace about everything that happens? For nothing can happen that can break a single one of these precious and exceeding great, supreme and wondrous promises.

What depth it gives to Peter's words when we remember that he was to die by crucifixion, and knew it. There is no promise of an easy passage, but there are countless promises for every day of the voyage, and for a welcome when He brings us to our desired haven (as Ps. 107:30 puts it).

Let us take one promise for our own today, live on it, test it and prove it — and thank Him for it.

❧

June 3

*And truly our fellowship is with the Father,
and with His Son Jesus Christ.
1 John 1:3*

Is this indeed true? Is this fellowship with the Father and the Son more real, more *used* than our fellowship with one another? It is so good to be together, to sing and pray and work together, that we may easily slip into finding our first joy there, rather than in that which alone gives vitality to the other.

Let us pray for those who have not the help of human fellowship, that there may be such a sense of the invisible, the spiritual, the blessed fellowship with the Father and with our Lord Jesus Christ, that all loss may be turned to gain.

And let us watch, lest in our joy in His gifts we ever become dependent upon one another.

O God, Thou art my God: early will I seek Thee. My soul thirsteth for Thee, my flesh also longeth after Thee (Ps: 63:1–2 BCP). *My soul hangeth upon Thee* (Ps. 63:9 BCP).

❧

June 4

He that loveth his brother abideth in the light,
and there is none occasion of stumbling in him.
1 John 2:10

"What an emphasis gets on kindness as life goes on," said Bishop Paget. Writing to someone in a Nursing Home, he said how he hoped the patient was "not too ill or weary to enjoy the happiness of feeling kindness all around you, and Goodness all above you."

As we watch the lives of those who have hearts "at leisure from themselves" and live for others, we cannot help seeing that there is "none occasion of stumbling" in them. They don't stumble people, they help them. They clear hindrances out of the path and make it much easier for those who do not know Him to find their Savior.

Let us more and more earnestly ask for this kindness of heart that shows itself in loving thoughts and deeds. Let us begin with ourselves. The Lord make us sensitive to the merest whisper of unlove in our hearts. *He that loveth . . . abideth.*

❧

June 5

For I the Lord thy God will hold thy right hand, saying unto
thee, Fear not; I will help thee. Fear not, thou worm.
Isa. 41:13–14

There is a feeling (I can only call it worminess) that
can come especially in the night. All the fight seems to
be drained out of you, and all power to endure. It is really a very horrid feeling, but the word of our wonderful
God is equal to anything — even to this. Last night,
through the sense of oppression and worminess, came
this: *Fear not, thou worm!*

Truly it was quite startling. It was so exactly right.
There was no smooth pretense that things were not
what they were. They were wormy. I was wormy. Well
then, *Fear not, thou worm!*

Our God meets us just where we are. But He does
not leave us there. There is power in the word of a King
to effect what it commands. In the *Fear not* of our God,
repeated from Genesis to Revelation, there is power to
give us just what we lack at that moment.

Rotherham translates that verse: "For I, thy God,
am firmly grasping thy right hand . . . am saying
unto thee, Do not fear. I have become thy helper. Do
not fear, thou worm."

Do not fear, but sing. *Praise the Lord upon*
earth . . . beasts and all cattle: WORMS (Ps. 148:7–10
BCP).

June 6

*Now I beseech you, brethren . . . that ye strive together
with me in your prayers to God for me; that I may be
delivered from them that do not believe in Judæa; and that
my service which I have for Jerusalem may be accepted of the
saints; that I may come unto you with joy by the will of God,
and may with you be refreshed.*
Rom. 15:30–32

*Our God whom we serve is able to deliver us. . . . But if not,
be it known unto thee, O king, that we will not serve thy
gods, nor worship the golden image which thou hast set up.*
Dan. 3:17–18

Paul asked his friends to strive together with him
against the dark powers about three things. Of the three,
one prayer we may conclude was answered according to
his expectations; the other two were not.

There was no joy, no refreshment for Paul in Rome
except the joy of being in the will of God.

May our faith, too, be of the Daniel 3:18 order.
That is triumph; that is faith. Nothing else is worthy of
the name.

Paul's glorious prison letters prove that he lived in
the spirit of these words. So should we.

❧

June 7

Thou winnowest my path and my lying down.
Ps. 139:3 *(margin)*

Young's literal translation is, *My path and my couch hast Thou fanned.* Could anything be more perfect? In the East the chaff is separated from the grain by fanning, so there is a double meaning in the word.

Whatever form the fan of the Lord takes (and it takes different forms according to His knowledge of the need of each), *whatever* the fan be, let us accept it with thanksgiving.

He shall baptize you with the Holy Ghost, and with fire: whose fan is in His hand, and He will thoroughly purge His floor, and gather His wheat into the garner (Matt. 3:11–12).

June 8

The lovingkindness of God lasteth all the day long.
Ps. 52:1 (Rotherham)

All the day long there is the pressure of life, and perhaps some inner strain to the spirit known only to God. But all the day long, too, there is the lovingkindness of God. And so all the day long the peace that passes all understanding.

It is a word small enough to remember easily. May it strengthen us all the moments of this day.

June 9

And God hath set some in the church, first apostles,
secondarily prophets, thirdly teachers, after that miracles,
then gifts of healings, helps, governments, diversities of
tongues. Are all apostles? are all prophets? are all teachers?
are all workers of miracles?
1 Cor. 12:28–29

"Helps and guidings," as Rotherham translates *gov-*
ernments, come sixth and seventh in the list in verse 28,
but do not recur in verse 29. Why?

This may be the reason. It is obvious that all are not
given gifts of apostleship and so on, but to all who live
close to their Lord two gifts are sure to be given.

These gifts are to help others, and to guide them
with peace.

Each one of us, however insignificant we may be,
can be a helper and a comforter. "And some there be
who keep themselves in peace and study to bring others
into peace."

June 10

Peace I leave with you, My peace I give unto you.
John 14:27

The peace of Jesus stood every sort of test, every strain, and it never broke. It is this, His very own peace, which He says *I give.* Do we take time to receive? A moment may be enough, but sometimes we need longer than that.

An alternative reading of 1 Corinthians 15:49 has a challenge for us. See the RV margin and Rotherham: *Even as we have borne the image of the man of earth, let us also bear the image of the man of heaven.*

What would He feel about this that fills our mind? What would He say? What would He do? *My peace I give unto you.* If we receive that peace we shall know the answer to these questions, and then by His touch upon us we shall bear the image of the man of heaven.

June 11

I therefore, the prisoner of the Lord...
Eph. 4:1

I have might for all things in Him that empowereth me.
Phil. 4:13 (Rotherham)

After the heights come the plains, in the Bible and in our everyday life. The glory and the wonder of the last verses of Ephesians 3 (the love of Christ, the fullness of God, Him that is able to do exceeding abundantly above all that we ask or think), are followed by *I . . . the prisoner of the Lord.*

There are strange limitations sometimes in our work itself. Sometimes we ourselves experience frustrations, inabilities, and chains known perhaps only to Him who knows all.

Paul opens the way of peace here, as he always does. It is acceptance. That crosses out all "ineffective unwillingness," and then all fret passes. There is peace.

June 12

Endeavoring to keep the unity of the Spirit
in the bond of peace.
Eph. 4:3

Forbearing one another, and forgiving each other . . . even as
the Lord forgave you, so also do ye: and above all these things
put on love, which is the bond of perfectness. And let the
peace of Christ rule in your hearts, to the which also ye were
called in one body; and be ye thankful.
Col. 3:13–15 (RV)

Endeavoring to keep the unity of the Spirit in
the bond of peace; *giving diligence; earnestly striving
to maintain.* Each translation emphasizes not the ease
of keeping in vital unity, but the difficulty. It is not a
natural thing for people to live so. It is supernatural,
heavenly. So it is assaulted on all sides by the Prince of
this world, sometimes covertly with a horrible subtlety,
sometimes openly. The underground operations of the
devil are more dangerous than the obvious attacks. But
Paul never contemplates defeat or any surrender whatever of the position, as Colossians 3:13–15 makes clear.
Nor need we.

ॐ

June 13

Neither pray I for these alone, but for them also which shall believe on Me through their word.
John 17:20

There is always attack upon prayer. How little we know of victory in that field. There is comfort for us in a sentence in the Episcopal Communion Service: "Not weighing our merits but pardoning our offences." There is still stronger comfort in the loving words of our Lord Jesus: *Neither pray I for these alone.* We begin our times of prayer as His pardoned and prayed-for ones, *made nigh by the blood of Christ* as Ephesians 2:13 tells us.

Sometimes, through illness or other causes, we find it hard to put our prayers into words. If prayer of the sort we long for is impossible, try giving up trying, and instead just let the Psalms or other great passages of Scripture turn themselves into prayers. "An inspired prayer implies an answer."

June 14

And the captain of the guard charged Joseph with them,
and he served them.
Gen. 40:4

Joseph was in prison. His feet were hurt with fet-
ters, his heart was hurt by injustice and unkindness. But
none of these things prevented him from helping others.

The story that follows shows how full of kindness
his service must have been. Joseph must have done more
than his bare duty. We do not go for sympathy to those
who have been cold and uninterested in our affairs. We
avoid them. The butler and the baker went to Joseph
sure of his loving, self-forgetful sympathy.

It makes us think of Another whose feet were hurt,
and His hands and His side, and far more His loving
heart. Out of the midst of His pains He thought of others, only of others.

Matthew 27:42: *He saved others; Himself He cannot
save.* More and more these words seem to sum up His
life on earth.

Lord Jesus, who left us an example that we should
follow in Thy steps, help us to follow. Let us forget self
in service. Give us Thy love that, loving others, loves
them to the end.

❧

June 15

*Light is sown for the righteous, and gladness for the upright
in heart. Rejoice in the Lord, ye righteous; and give thanks
at the remembrance of His holiness.*
Ps. 97:11–12

Some of us, perhaps, have mentally passed on to others the promise of Psalm 97:11, but not felt it belonged to us because we could not class ourselves among the righteous and upright. Yet in His wonderful love the Lord has continually done for us what we know we do not deserve.

Verse 12 of Psalm 97 illuminates verse 11. Is there one of us who cannot rejoice in Him who loved us and gave Himself for us? The least of us can rejoice in Him and give thanks as we remember His holiness.

It is very wonderful that all He asks of us is this — this that we cannot help doing when we see our Lord. He says: "If only you will turn your eyes from yourself to Me, your God and your eternal Lover, then I shall be free to sow My shining seeds on either side of your path, so that you will walk in it gathering flowers of gladness all the way."

Nothing can shut up His hand from sowing seeds of light. As we go on, doing the will of our Father quite irrespective of personal likes and dislikes, we shall find that He sows these seeds overnight. By dawn there is a springing up of new green things, and long before the sun is hot the buds have opened into flowers. Don't let us miss these flowers. Let us enjoy them and give them to others.

June 16

*Thus saith the Lord, which giveth the sun for a light by day,
and the ordinances of the moon and of the stars for a light by
night, which divideth the sea when the waves thereof roar;
the Lord of hosts is His name: If those ordinances depart
from before Me, saith the Lord, then the seed of Israel also
shall cease from being a nation before Me for ever. Thus
saith the Lord: If heaven above can be measured, and the
foundations of the earth searched out beneath,
I will also cast off all the seed of Israel for all that
they have done, saith the Lord.*
Jer. 31:35–37

Here is a glorious word for those who are tempted
to feel that God cannot go on loving one who is so unworthy to be loved.

Does the sun shine? Do the moon and stars give
light by night? Those ordinances have not yet departed.
Then we have not yet ceased to be dear to Him.

Can we measure the heaven above or search out the
foundations of the earth beneath? Then we are not cast
off in spite of all that we have done and all that we are.

Jeremiah 31:3, *Yea, I have loved thee with an everlasting love,* means that. John 13:1, *Having loved His
own which were in the world, He loved them unto the end,*
means that. Blessed be the eternal love of God.

June 17

The steps of a good man are ordered by the Lord:
and he delighteth in his way.
Ps. 37:23

The Lord therefore hath performed His word
that He hath spoken.
2 Chron. 6:10

Praise God for His guidance! Here is a chorus to sing:

Thou hast performed the thing that Thou hast spoken;
    Guided our steps and shown us what to do;
Never, O Lord, hath word of Thine been broken;
    Thou art the Truth, and we have proved Thee true.

June 18

*Then spake the Lord to Paul in the night by a vision, Be
not afraid, but speak, and hold not thy peace: for I am with
thee, and no man shall set on thee to hurt thee:
for I have much people in this city.*
Acts 18:9–10

"I would commend the reader to the gentle love
of God," wrote Jacob Boehme. Acts 18:9–10 shows the
Lord's "gentle love" in meeting us just where we are,
and saying the one word we most need. Paul, dreading
a repetition of the many stripes (perhaps the wounds
were not quite healed), is comforted by a promise that
he will not be hurt. And *be not afraid* — carry on — *for
I am with you.*

It is worthwhile to watch for these special private
words. They come in all sorts of unexpected ways.

June 19

Jesus answered and said unto him, What I do thou knowest
not now; but thou shalt know hereafter.
John 13:7

Blessed are ye, when men shall revile you, and persecute you,
and shall say all manner of evil against you falsely,
for My sake.
Matt. 5:11

In Acts 16 we read how Paul was forbidden by the
Holy Spirit to go to preach the word in Asia (v. 6) and in
Bithynia (v. 7), but had a vision of a man saying, *Come*
over into Macedonia, and help us. And immediately they
set out, *assuredly gathering that the Lord had called us for*
to preach the gospel unto them (vv. 9–10).

The result was bad trouble; they were beaten, cast
into prison, and put in the stocks. It must have been
very perplexing for them.

To the questions that come about things we know
the Lord does (vv. 6 and 7), the answer of peace is found
in John 13:7. To the opposite kind of question, about
things the devil does (v. 20 onwards), we have Matthew
5:11.

This distinction holds good every time. In this one
chapter of Acts we have opportunities for both kinds of
questions, exactly as in one short period of life we may
find ourselves faced with both.

But there is always peace in these two answers.

They explain nothing, but they still the heart and lead it into quietness.

That is why at midnight Paul and Silas were able to sing praises to God; and we know what happened after that.

June 20

Zebulun shall dwell at the haven of the sea;
and he shall be for an haven of ships.
Gen. 49:13

Zebulun — an haven. From Judah (the fourth son) to Zebulun (the tenth) the Spirit, guiding Jacob's words, led him on. There are interesting historical fulfillments of all these prophecies, but today we will consider something very simple and yet very searching.

Zebulun offered a haven of refuge to the Lion of the tribe of Judah when, as a little child, He was brought home from Egypt. And Zebulun gave Him all His disciples except Judas.

How few havens have been prepared for Him who is still the rejected of men; how few welcomes wait for Him anywhere. Can the loving Spirit say of our home — "an haven"? Can our dear Lord say of our hearts, "I will rest in My love there today"?

Judas grudged the ointment of spikenard, very costly, which Mary poured on the feet that were so soon to be wounded for her and for us. But Judas was not of Zebulun. Can our Lord Jesus count on us to be His men of Zebulun who love with the love that sets no limitations, keeps nothing back?

June 21

*Then I said, I have labored in vain, I have spent my strength
for nought, and in vain: yet surely my judgment
is with the Lord, and my reward with my God.
Isa. 49:4 (margin)*

*Is it not lawful for Me to do what I will with Mine own?
Matt. 20:15*

Is it not lawful for Him to do what He wills with
His own? Is it not lawful for Him to allow us to wait on
in faith? Is it not lawful for Him to allow His own to be
disappointed? Of course it is.

This covers everything: all toil apparently (not really) spent in vain, all disappointments, all seeming failure.

"To what purpose have I toiled? For waste and mist
my vigor have I spent" (Isa. 49:4 Rotherham) is a Calvary word. But there is a triumphant end to it: "And my
God be proved to have been my strength."

Later when we look back we shall see the unexplained things of life shine like jewels. We shall see that
nothing was lost, nothing really was wasted. There is no
such thing as "love's labor lost" with Him.

Till then — *Is it not lawful for Me to do what I will
with Mine own?* Yes, Lord.

June 22

And Joseph called the name of the firstborn Manasseh
[Forgetting]: For God, said he, hath made me forget all my
toil. . . . And the name of the second called he Ephraim
[Fruitful]: For God hath caused me to be fruitful
in the land of my affliction.
Gen. 41:51–52

Forgetting those things which are behind, and reaching forth
unto those things which are before, I press toward the mark.
Phil. 3:13–14

"Forgetting; fruitful." The word "forgetting" takes
us to Philippians 3:13. As we grow older the adversary
reminds us of how much more we used to do, of things
we cannot do now, of joys we must lay down. The word
of release then is "Forgetting, reaching forth, I press on."

There are times when we are tempted to remember
and brood over the trials of the past. Sometimes we feel
broken-hearted over unkind words and misunderstand-
ings. It helps then to remember our dear Lord's words
(Ps. 35:11): *False witnesses did rise up; they laid to My*
charge things that I knew not. Let us never forget what
He said to His disciples after He had washed their feet,
The servant is not greater than his lord (John 13:16).

As we, by His grace, "forget" and reach forth and
press on, He turns our forgetting into fruitfulness. The
sap in us is free to flow, not round and round ourselves,
but out into leaf and bud and flower and fruit, to His
glory and to the help of others.

❧

June 23

And Israel stretched out his right hand, and laid it upon
Ephraim's head, who was the younger, and his left hand
upon Manasseh's head, guiding his hands wittingly;
for Manasseh was the firstborn.
Gen. 48:14

So he . . . guided them by the skillfulness of his hands.
Ps. 78:72

"Guiding his hands wittingly." Do we ever read this story without thinking of the mean and faithless scheming of Genesis 27? Israel must have thought of it. He must have felt humbly and sorrowfully how needless it all was.

There is a wonderful sense of release when we understand that we need never plan for ourselves, never try to twist circumstances so that our wishes shall come to pass. We have only one thing to do, such a happy, peaceful thing that we can never be glad enough and grateful enough for it. We have only to commit ourselves and our ways to Him who guides us by the skillfulness of His Hands.

June 24

More to be desired are they than gold, yea,
than much fine gold.
Ps. 19:10

When we go to services or meetings, let us listen with keen expectation to what our God, who knows exactly what our need is, has prepared for us. When the pure gold of the word of God is given, it lays a great responsibility on all who listen, lest they lose that precious thing. We cannot afford to lose one word.

If someone opened a bag of gold coins and poured them out, saying, "Take what you can," would there be any slackness about picking up those coins? But these words of God are more to be desired than gold, yes, than much fine gold.

❧

June 25

*And the angel of the Lord appeared unto him in a flame of
fire out of the midst of a bush: and he looked, and, behold,
the bush burned with fire, and the bush was not consumed.
And Moses said, I will now turn aside, and see this great
sight, why the bush is not burnt. . . .
And God said unto Moses, I AM THAT I AM.
Exod. 3:2–3, 14*

Rotherham's rendering of the great words of the
KJV are, "I will Become whatsoever I please." And his
note is: "What He will be is left unexplained. He will be
Helper, Strengthener, Deliverer."

God's choice of the scrubby thorn bush, the "nothing" of His creation, reminds us of Paul's words in 1
Corinthians 1:26–31 about our calling. God has chosen
foolish things, weak things, things which are despised
and even things which are not, *that no flesh should glory
in His presence.*

Lord, we are Thy thorn bushes, Thy nothings. O
Fire of Love Eternal, Become whatsoever Thou pleasest,
and keep us Thy humble thorn bushes growing in the
dust at Thy feet.

❧

June 26

And Moses said unto the Lord, O my Lord,
I am not eloquent.
Exod. 4:10

They think that they shall be heard for their much speaking.
Be not ye therefore like unto them.
Matt. 6:7–8

These are words of comfort for those whose chief work is prayer. Prayer is greatly helped by loved companionship — "loved" because the least hurt to love wounds prayer. When John wrote *Beloved, let us love one another: for love is of God; and everyone that loveth is born of God, and knoweth God,* he was leading on to that wonderful word about prayer, *And this is the confidence that we have in Him, that, if we ask anything according to His will, He heareth us* (1 John 4:7; 5:14).

Even the most alone of us is one of a wonderful Companionship. The Spirit is making intercession, and Christ our Lord ever liveth to make intercession, so we are not alone even when we seem to be alone.

We do not have to be eloquent. We do not need to speak much. We do not even need to know what we should pray for. "For His compassion matches our yearning — is ever taking our human frailty by the hand. We are not even sure what boons should rightly be the object of our prayers; but His Spirit — His very Spirit — is pleading ever for us with sighings such as no language can shape into words. . . . His Spirit intercedes for His hallowed ones in just the way that God desires" (Rom. 8:26–27 Way).

❧

June 27

Father, if Thou be willing, remove this cup from Me:
nevertheless not My will, but Thine, be done.
Luke 22:42

Bathed round about by moonlit air,
    Beneath the olive tree,
Our Savior knelt alone in prayer;
    Sore spent was He.

And solemn through the moonlit air
    The prayer of prayers arose;
But what it cost to pray that prayer
    No mortal knows.

Only our hearts within us know
    When they most broken be,
To that same garden we must go —
    Gethsemane.

And only one prayer meets our need,
    We learn to pray it there;
The prayer of all true prayers the seed,
    Our Savior's prayer.

June 28

God . . . is able to do exceeding abundantly above all
that we ask or think.
Eph. 3:19–20

"Few suspect what God would do in their souls, if only they would let Him do it." That word was fulfilled in the life of the one who wrote it. When St. Ignatius had to face death by torture he said: "Let me be given to the wild beasts, for through them I can attain unto God. I am God's wheat, and I am ground by the wild beasts that I may be found the pure bread of Christ."

It is one thing to face pain when it is not near but some distance off and there is just a hope that it may not have to be. It is quite another to face it when it is near and there is no escape from it. It was near to that old man, and it was terrific. And then those who looked on saw what God had done in a soul that was wholly yielded up to Him.

How ashamed such a story makes us. If we have failed in the trifles of life, the little trials that are sometimes allowed to come to us, it can only be because we have not let God do all He would in our souls if He had full right of way.

June 29

Greater love hath no man than this, that a man lay down his life for his friends.
John 15:13

Hereby know we love, because He laid down His life for us: and we ought to lay down our lives for the brethren. But whoso hath the world's goods, and beholdeth his brother in need, and shutteth up his compassion from him, how doth the love of God abide in him? . . . Let us not love in word, neither with the tongue; but in deed and truth.
1 John 3:16–18 (RV)

These verses are often quoted as referring to a death for others, but the first thought in our Lord's mind must have been of a life laid down in loving service. The life that does not shut up its compassion but loves in deed — in the doing of real things — this is first of all the life laid down.

The inspiration for that life is not only Calvary but all the years before. Our Lord's patience throughout those years, going on loving in spite of disappointments and ungratefulness, how that challenges us who find disappointment and ingratitude so trying. Think of the courage that could trust heavenly matters to those poor human hands. Even His nearest and dearest wrangled about who would be greatest during His very last meal with them. And yet His love could overlook everything and say of such followers, *They have kept Thy word* (John

17:6). He knew, as only Love can know, that in spite of all failures *that* was their heart's desire. And so He spoke of them at their highest, not their lowest.

Lord, evermore give us *this* love, that we may lay down our lives for the brethren.

June 30

He is altogether lovely. This is my Beloved,
and this is my Friend.
Song of Sol. 5:16

What is thy Beloved more than another beloved? (v. 9). That was the question asked of one who was so unworthy of her Beloved that she had grieved Him until He had to withdraw Himself from her. She sought Him but she could not find Him. She called Him, but He gave her no answer. It could not be otherwise, for her thoughts were moving round herself so that there was no room for Him.

But now she forgets herself in thinking of Him and showing Him to others. She cannot find words beautiful enough to show Him worthily. *He is altogether lovely,* she says. *THIS is my Beloved, and THIS is my Friend.* And instantly she is with Him in spirit. She knows where He is. There is no more separation.

There is nothing that can surprise our Lord in our unworthiness; He knows us through and through. But it must surprise Him sometimes that we ever stay even for one minute in the dark and cold, when we have such a Beloved and such a Friend that we have only to think of Him (instead of ourselves) to find ourselves with Him, embraced by His warm love on every side.

❧

July 1

Then shall we know, if we follow on to know the Lord:
His going forth is prepared as the morning.
Hos. 6:3

Prepare to meet thy God.
Amos 4:12

The Septuagint renders Hosea 6:3: *We shall find Him ready as the morning,* ready to meet us and bless us as the sunrise is ready every morning to bless the world.

But before there could be dawn in this world of ours, tremendous things had to happen in space. It was not a little thing to God to create a dawn. And in the spiritual world tremendous things had to be, before our darkness could be enlightened by the Eternal Dawn. Calvary had to happen. Calvary was God's preparation for our Sunrise.

Is it much, then, that He should ask for preparation from us? *Prepare to meet thy God,* today and every day. Prepare to meet Him whom we shall find "ready as the morning."

❧

July 2

And who then is willing to consecrate his service
this day unto the Lord?
1 Chron. 29:5

Yad, the Hebrew word translated "service," also means *hands.* There is very little that we do without using our hands. It is these hands, not something spiritual and intangible, but these our own hands of flesh and blood, that the Lord asks us to consecrate to Him today. To take this literally is to hallow everything.

God asks for *my* hands. Lord Jesus, here they are. Cleanse them and keep them clean for Thy use today.

❧

July 3

Do Thou for me, O God the Lord, for Thy name's sake.
Ps. 109:21

There are times when we do not know what to pray for as we ought. It is restful, then, to leave the matter open. *Do Thou for me, O God the Lord.* That covers my personal need. *Do Thou for them* covers the need of those I love. It does not matter that I do not know how to pray for them as I want to pray. He knows everything, and He will do for them all that His love sees is best.

Rotherham's translation of 2 Chronicles 20:20 has a word of joy for us all: *Trust ye in the Lord your God and ye shall be trusted.* We shall be trusted with answers to prayer which are not what we desired, as well as with those which are. Isn't it wonderful to be trusted like that, with just anything?

❧

July 4

And we know that all things work together for good to them
that love God, to them who are the called
according to His purpose.
Rom. 8:28

Romans 8:28 contains a certainty which the great adversary continually assaults. It was so with Joseph. First at Dothan, then in Egypt, all things seemed to be working together for harm, not good. We read of no special revelation granted for his help in prison. He seems to have been trusted to walk by faith not by sight, as for the most part we are too.

Joseph had not his own finished story to read, nor Romans 8:28, nor any other scripture. If we try to imagine life without a Bible we can only marvel at the wonder of the grace of God shown forth in Joseph and in countless others, right up to today.

Samuel Rutherford wrote about those who seem to be our enemies: "They are set to work as undersmiths and servants to the work of refining the saints. Their office is to scour and cleanse vessels for the King's table." Thank God for this certainty. The effect of man's sin or mistake, temptation to discouragement about ourselves, all limitations and frustrations, and all trials of the flesh and spirit, are really "undersmiths and servants" working together for good to us who love God.

And this is true, too, of all the thousands of joys we experience — they too are God's servants working together for our good.

July 5

I do set My bow in the cloud, and it shall be for a token of
a covenant between Me and the earth. And it shall come to
pass, when I bring a cloud over the earth,
that the bow shall be seen in the cloud.
Gen. 9:13–14

Is it cloudy weather for any of us? When it is, don't
let us miss our rainbows. They are for a token of the
covenant between God and us. God the Father whose
name is Love, whose will is love, set His rainbow in the
clouds to remind us of that love.

Don't let us be surprised at inward trials of faith,
patience, joy, peacefulness and humility. Is the *I* in us
killed in a day? Are we made perfect in a day? The cloud
that makes the pastures green is a good cloud. The rainbow of the love of God is set in every cloud that ever
darkens our sky. Clouds and rainbows work together for
the perfecting of our souls.

July 6

He setteth an end to darkness, and searcheth out all
perfection. . . . He cutteth out rivers among the rocks;
and His eye seeth every precious thing.
Job 28:3, 10

Why do ye not understand My speech? even
because ye cannot hear My word.
John 8:43

"So you will ride at ease over the breakers of this
mortal life, and not care too much what befalls you —
not from carelessness but from the soaring gladness of
heavenly love," wrote Janet Erskine Stuart. But sometimes the breakers can seem rather breaking, and then
words of Job can help.

He setteth an end to darkness. This will not go on
forever.

He cutteth out rivers among the rocks. Often one can
only see rocks and jungle, but the river is there. We can
hear its flowing.

Let us take comfort from the thought of the *end*.
Our God setteth an *end* to every kind of darkness. The
morning comes, a morning without clouds. We are facing towards the morning all the time.

Till then, while we are still in darkness, and in the
place where we can see nothing but rocks, let us find our
way to the riverbed and drink of the water He gives us,
and go on our way refreshed.

The Lord help us to hear His word, that we may understand His speech and miss nothing of what He has to give us day by day.

July 7

O spare me, that I may recover strength. (Kay):
That I may smile again.
Ps. 39:13

The Lord . . . that strengtheneth the spoiled against the
strong, so that the spoiled shall come against the fortress.
Amos 5:8–9

According to Young, the Hebrew word *balag* used
in these two verses means "to brighten up, encourage,
comfort." It is a lovely prayer to use when we feel weary
and dull. "Lord, brighten me up; encourage me."

All of us who are fighting the Lord's battles know
only too well what it is to appear as the spoiled before
the strong. Here is His promise for us then. The Lord
will strengthen us so that the fortress will be taken and
the Lord Himself will triumph. What more could we
want?

July 8

Our God is a consuming fire.
Heb. 12:29

I will turn My hand upon thee, and purely purge away thy
dross, and take away all thy tin.
Isa. 1:25

He will thoroughly purge His floor, and gather His wheat
into the garner; but He will burn up the chaff
with unquenchable fire.
Matt. 3:12

More and more we learn to fear and hate our dross.
We do not want our husks. We want to be pure gold,
pure grain. Thank God that His fire is unquenchable.

Deuteronomy 33:2–3 tells us *From His right hand*
went a fiery law for them. Yea, He loved the people. And
Rotherham translates Song of Solomon 8:6–7, *Love is*
strong as death. The flames thereof are flames of fire — the
flash of JEHOVAH. Many waters cannot drown love.

Love like that will not fail. It is equal to all it will
cost Him to purge and purify even such as we are. Our
God is a consuming Fire — consuming Love.

O Lord our God, to Thee is known
    Our inmost heart's desire;
Thy love is fire, Thy love alone;
    O bathe our souls in fire.

❧

July 9

The name of the first is Pison: that is it which compasseth the whole land of Havilah, where there is gold; and the gold of that land is good.
Gen. 2:11–12

And the city was pure gold, like unto clear glass.
Rev. 21:18

The first mention of gold in Genesis, and the last in Revelation, are full of a lovely thought. Our Havilah may be just an ordinary patch of earth, but if the gold of that land be good, when we come to the City we shall find something familiar, only glorified. It will not be a strange place to us.

The noun which is often used for gold is derived from a root meaning "shining." We know what makes a place to shine: it is *the kindness and love of God our Savior.* That golden phrase occurs in a dark setting, Titus 3:3–4: *We ourselves also were sometimes foolish, disobedient, deceived . . . living in malice and envy, hateful, and hating one another. But after that the kindness and love of God our Savior toward man appeared.* "Appeared" here means "to shine upon." So we have the thought of kindness and love shining upon us, and we (in contrast to days past) shining too with kindness and love, rich in the gold of the Lord of Love. *And the gold of that land is good.*

Let us set our hearts upon this more earnestly than ever, so that everyone coming near us will feel the shining of that love.

❧

July 10

*Shiggaion [a song] of David, which he sang unto the Lord,
concerning the words of Cush the Benjamite.*
Ps. 7 Title

*O Lord my God, in Thee do I put my trust: save me from all
them that persecute me, and deliver me.* Ps. 7:1

*I will praise the Lord according to His righteousness: and
will sing praise to the name of the Lord most high.*
Ps. 7:17

Cush is mentioned in the title of Psalm 7, and we
see that disagreeable person doing exactly as people
sometimes do to us. We see, too, what we should do
when distressed by them. David sang unto the Lord. He
told Him all about it and then he turned from it and
sang those happy words at the end of the psalm, *I will
praise the Lord according to His righteousness: and I will
sing praise to the name of the Lord most high.*

If a Cush springs up among us, with his unkind
and untrue accusations, let us try David's way. According to Matthew 5:23–24 the first thing to do is to go to
Cush and try to get things straight. If that fails, the right
thing to do is not to discuss it with others, or to be miserable about it, brooding over it in a dreadful gloomy
silence. The right thing is to sing.

The wicked pleasure of hurting another is hateful,
devilish. Cush means *Black*. The Lord make us white all
through, like those of whom it is written in Revelation
3:4, *They shall walk with Me in white: for they are worthy.*

July 11

If there be first a willing mind, it is accepted according to that a man hath, and not according to that he hath not.
2 Cor. 8: 12

In Sir William Bragg's *World of Sound* he writes of our English scale of music, with its twelve intervals. We know what great music has been made from this scale. The old Gaelic scale had fewer notes, and yet music has been made out of it too. "Auld Lang Syne" is written in this scale. It can be played on the black keys alone.

Some of us have twelve notes to offer to God. Thank God for them. *What hast thou that thou didst not receive?* (1 Cor. 4:7). Offer them all, and God will play His great music through your life.

Some of us have only five notes to offer. Don't let us be discouraged. God can make eternal music out of only five notes.

July 12

[Love] thinketh no evil.
1 Cor. 13:5

Nor taketh up a reproach against his neighbor.
Ps. 15:3

If all of us, by the grace of God, lived in the spirit of these two verses it would set free an immense amount of time and strength for the Things of the Father, that Business for which alone we Christians are in the world. Think of the time that would be set free for prayer for those who do not know Him, if we had not to spend so much on those who do. Think of the strength we have to expend in sorting out wrong relationships, which could be given instead to the War of the Lord.

It should be simply impossible for us to think unkindly of anyone. Satan will always see to it that there are people ready to sow seeds of suspicion. Let us refuse to receive them. Let us not endure them for a moment. Let us not imagine evil in our heart, but always put the best and most loving construction on everything. Unkindness in our thought life is one of the things that God hates. *Beloved, let us love* (1 John 4:7).

July 13

Let brotherly love continue. Heb. 13:1

Now the God of peace, that brought again from the dead our Lord Jesus, that great Shepherd of the sheep, through the blood of the everlasting covenant, make you perfect in every good work to do His will, working in you that which is wellpleasing in His sight, through Jesus Christ.
Heb. 13:20–21

There will be many things in our prayers today, but let us give five minutes for God to tell us what He thinks about kindness. Will five minutes be enough? We may find we need longer.

Now the God of peace make you perfect . . . to do His will. Are we perfect in kindness? Peter tells us, as though we need to be reminded of it, to add kindness to godliness (2 Pet. 1:7). Paul writes, in Weymouth's translation of Colossians 3:12, *Clothe yourselves therefore, as God's own people, holy and dearly loved, with tenderheartedness, kindness.* Here again holiness and kindness are set together.

Are we living according to this, the revealed desire of our God? Do we want to please Him more perfectly "by kindness"? Then let us sweep away any thought of unkindness that may be lingering in any corner of our heart.

Let us ask Him, whose dearest name is Love, to fill our hearts so full of love today that kindness will flow out all the time, and never anything else.

❧

July 14

Hear me when I call, O God of my righteousness:
Thou hast enlarged me when I was in distress;
have mercy upon me and hear my prayer.
Ps. 4:1

A snail which appeared to be dead was fixed to a tablet in the British Museum and kept there for four years. One day someone noticed that it had a new door (epiphragm is the scientific name). This was astonishing. He took the snail off the tablet and put it into warm water and it revived and came out of its shell. Next day it had a meal of cabbage and began to mend its somewhat broken shell.

No snail that ever was created would choose to be fixed on a tablet in the British Museum. Some of us sometimes feel "fixed on a tablet," when we are not able to do what we naturally wish to do. The snail has a fine word for us.

There is just one way of peace for those who want to be good snails. It is much easier to write of it than to do it, but (Phil. 4:13) *Through Christ which strengtheneth me* can make it possible. Take Rotherham's version of Psalm 4:1, *In a strait place Thou hast made room for me,* and till the day of "enlargement" comes, be contented with the strait place — like that snail.

July 15

Counsel is Mine and sound wisdom:
I am understanding; I have strength.
Prov. 8:14

God understandeth the way thereof
and He knoweth the place thereof.
Job 28:23:

God understands. There are no ways and no places that He does not understand.

Have you ever thought what a tremendous difference it would make to our lives if this were not true? Imagine the feelings of a soldier if he had good reason to doubt that his commanding officer understood the situation. We are soldiers. Our Commander understands. *His understanding is infinite* (Ps. 147:5). *Though war should rise against me, in this will I be confident* (Ps. 27:3).

Because of His infinite understanding, God knows that we want to be sure that the One who says He understands has been through the mill Himself. And so we have this wonderful touch of His special understanding in Proverbs 8, where it is clear that the speaker is our Lord Jesus Christ Himself. *I am Understanding.* I, the Man of Sorrows acquainted with grief, I who was tempted in all points just as you are, I am Understanding.

It is restful to be understood, to be with one who never misjudges. Let us rest in His presence today.

๛

July 16

*For God is not unrighteous to forget your work and labor of
love, which ye have showed toward His name,
in that ye have ministered to the saints, and do minister.*
Heb. 6:10

This is the special word for all who do the business
of a household: housekeepers, cooks, room-cleaners and
others. It is a word also for those who plan pleasure for
others, givers of flowers, writers of letters, all unseen un-
sung office workers, and all who serve in any way. The
only thing that matters is that our service should not just
be something done because it has to be done, but what
the Spirit of God calls a *labor of love.*

Among the myriad of things held in the memory
of our Heavenly Father are these little inconspicuous
things, *your work and labor of love.*

July 17

O Lord God . . . I pray Thee, send me good speed this day.
Gen. 24:12

But when ye pray, use not vain repetitions, as the heathen
do: for they think that they shall be heard for their much
speaking. Be not ye therefore like unto them: for your Father
knoweth what things ye have need of, before ye ask Him.
Matt. 6:7–8

Our Lord told His disciples that there was no need for many words when they prayed. A brief prayer goes straight to the heart of God. Abraham's servant teaches us a prayer we can pray at all times, however pressed for time we may be. It covers everything. *O Lord God, send me good speed this day.* Give me success today, in my prayer life, in my work, in what I think and say and do, in what I am.

It is a telegram prayer. Let us use it at moments of sudden need. We know it will be answered, for "our Father knows" our needs long before we ask Him.

❧

July 18

Deal Thou unto me, O Lord God, according unto Thy Name; for sweet is Thy mercy.
Ps. 109:20 (BCP)

The Psalms give us many brief telegram prayers, and here is another we can use today. *Deal Thou with me according unto Thy Name.*

We can use it, too, for all in need, and especially for the ill.

> Deal Thou with them, O God the Lord,
>   Deal Thou with them;
> According to Thy Name of Love,
>   Deal Thou with them.
> The floods that else would overflow,
>   Rebuke and stem.
>
> Sweet is Thy mercy, God the Lord,
>   And we have *proved*
> That mercy sweet. O God of Love,
>   Thy well-beloved
> Are ill and need Thee. Deal with them,
>   Thine own beloved.

July 19

I hate every false way.
Ps. 119:128

I hate and abhor lying.
Ps. 119:163

We must be alert to notice the beginnings of loose thinking about Truth. Suppose a question is asked, "Did such and such a thing happen?" and the one who is questioned is not sure but thinks it did. To reply "Yes" is to tell a lie. To say "I don't know" may show carelessness where care was expected, but it is truth, and truth is golden.

"She gave to everybody an immediate sense of truth such as we have when a sum comes right." May that be a true description of each one of us. But if anyone feels, "That cannot be said of me," here is a word of hope. In Luke 13:11–13 we read of the woman who had been crooked for eighteen years, but when the Lord laid His hands on her *immediately she was made straight.* He who straightened that crooked body can straighten the crooked soul of anyone who wants to have it done. Then that one will find a horror of every false way growing stronger every day, till he or she can honestly say, *I hate every false way. I hate and abhor lying; but Thy law do I love.*

❧

July 20

Who through faith…out of weakness were made strong.
Heb. 11:33–34

Long ago a toy was invented in Holland, which Prince Rupert brought to England. These toys were bubbles of glass, and were called Rupert's drops. Molten glass was dropped into water, and took the form of a tadpole. The body part could stand quite a hard knock, but the least tap broke the tail. If even the tip of the tail were broken, the whole tadpole flew into fine dust of glass, "with explosive noise."

Most of us know what it is to feel rather like those tadpoles. "I can bear this and this and this," we say, "but I really can't stand that!" Touch our tails and — well, we may have learned not to "go off in explosive violence," but even so there is something uncommonly like the shattering of the glass ball.

What we need is to be made powerful inwardly, so that we can resist at all points, even when our tail is touched. And this is the very promise we have in Hebrews 11:34.

Nearly everyone has some special fear, something more dreaded than anything else. The men and women of old were just the same as we are, and yet they did not give way, for *out of weakness they were made strong inwardly.* The God who did that for them can do the same for us. We need not have tadpole tails.

❧

July 21

Then I said, I have labored in vain, I have spent my strength for nought, and in vain: yet surely my judgment is with the Lord, and my work [or, my reward] with my God.
Isa. 49:4

The second clause of that verse can strengthen us when we are discouraged. The Speaker is our Lord Himself, who was tempted in all points like as we are — even in this point. He is touched with the feeling of our infirmities, and is able to succor us who are tempted.

Look at the summing up of all in Philippians 2:16, which Way renders thus: *So shall I exult in anticipation of the Day of Messiah's coming, in the thought that I have not run my race for a phantom prize, nor toiled for an elusive wage.*

Lay these glorious words in the storehouse of memory, so that when the devil comes as he came to our Lord and has come and will come to all His followers, he may find you prepared. And should he say, "Yes, but you are not St. Paul," meet him with another word from the same letter (2:13): *For it is God which worketh in you both to will and to do of His good pleasure.* Alleluia! For it is God.

❧

July 22

Strengthened with all might, according to His glorious power,
unto all patience and long-suffering with joyfulness.
Col. 1:11

Sometimes nothing helps us more than to read and re-read some great word of our God's. We can renew our strength by reading it not just in one version, but in many. Each yields some new emphasis, some fresh light.

Colossians 1:11 is a fathomless word. Ponder these different translations.

Moffatt: "May His glorious might nerve you with full power to endure and to be patient cheerfully, whatever comes."

Weymouth: "Since His power is so glorious, may you be strengthened with strength of every kind, and be prepared for cheerfully enduring all things with patience and longsuffering."

Way: "I ask Him that with all His strength you may be strengthened, even to the measure of the might of His divine majesty, till you attain to all-enduring patience and forbearance, which exults under suffering."

The devil will see to it that there is something to try the spirit today. He always sharpens his fiery darts. But he can do nothing against this shield.

❧

July 23

According to the gospel of the glory of the blessed God.
1 Tim. 1:11 (RV)

Rotherham gives us a lovely version of this verse: *According to the glad message of the glory of the happy God.*

Can we ever thank Him enough for the Spirit of happiness, which comes from the happy God? Often sorrowful psalms are followed by joyful ones. Even sorrowful verses are often followed by glad ones, as in Psalm 102:11–12: *My days are like a shadow that declineth; and I am withered like grass. BUT THOU, O Lord, shalt endure for ever; and Thy remembrance unto all generations.*

So let us rejoice today in the glad message of the glory of the Happy God.

July 24

Out of the north cometh golden splendor.
Job 37:22 (RV)

We may hear our Lord's words in Elihu's words to Job, for in the Song of Solomon 4:16 it is surely He who says, *Awake, O north wind; and come, thou south; blow upon My garden, that the spices thereof may flow out.* And we respond, *Let my Beloved come into His garden, and eat His pleasant fruits.*

If the north wind seems to be blowing in our garden today, let us take heart. Never does He call the north wind, or any other wind, to blow upon His garden without coming Himself. Then there is fair weather whatever wind may blow.

Out of the north cometh golden splendor (RV).
Fair weather cometh out of the north (KJV).

For He is our Fair Weather.

July 25

*Meditate upon these things; give thyself wholly to them;
that thy profiting may appear to all.*
1 Tim. 4:15

This is a quotation from C.F. Holder's *Louis Agassiz* (the great authority on fishes): "He could not bear with superficial study — a man should give his whole life to the object he had undertaken to investigate. He felt that desultory, isolated, spasmodic working avails nothing, but curses with narrowness and mediocrity."

Put that beside 1 Timothy 4:15. "Habitually practice these duties, and be absorbed in them" (Weymouth). "Let them be the atmosphere of your life, in order that your spiritual growth may be evident to all" (Way).

Spiritual growth depends upon study, concentration, determination. Let us take to heart today further words Paul wrote to Timothy, in his second letter, chapter 3, verses 14–17. Way's version of part of that passage is: "Abide by the lessons you have learned: hold to your convictions.... Every written record inspired by God is also helpful for teaching truth, for refuting error, for restoration of the lapsed, for training in righteousness, so that the man of God may be thorough, may be perfectly equipped for all good work."

❧

July 26

He shall drink of the brook in the way:
therefore shall He lift up the head.
Ps. 110:7

We think of our Lord as Savior, Shepherd, Master, Guide and King, but have you ever thought of Him as a mountaineer? The word in Psalm 110:7 should be translated "torrent" — mountain torrent. A mountain torrent, of course, flows down a mountain, and that means that the one who drinks of it is climbing the mountain.

Kay's note is: "He shall not faint in the long and weary conflict. As He journeys on, He drinks of a wayside mountain torrent — the river of truth and righteousness — and so advances on His career of victory.

"The 22nd Canon of the Second Council of Orange says: 'Whatever of truth and righteousness man has, is from that fountain, after which we in this desert ought to thirst, in order that, *bedewed as it were with a few drops from it, we may not faint in the way.*' From that fountain the King of Righteousness had a full torrent accompanying Him throughout His progress."

That same torrent flows for us today as we climb our mountains.

❧

July 27

I will seek that which was lost, and bring again that which was driven away, and will bind up that which was broken, and will strengthen that which was sick.
Ezek. 34:16

Perhaps when we read those words our hearts are sad over some who do not seem to want to be brought back, and bound up and strengthened. It helps, if we remember that this is first and foremost His sorrow. Our feeling it, too, means that we do not leave Him to sorrow alone, as He was left to pray alone in the garden of Gethsemane.

So let us not give up hope, for He never does. Even if we have prayed for someone for many years without seeing any result, let us continue steadfastly. We know that the Good Shepherd goes on seeking His lost sheep *until He finds*.

July 28

In Thy presence is fullness of joy.
Ps. 16:11

"By the practice of the Presence of God, by steadfast gaze on Him, the soul comes to the knowledge of God, full and deep, to an Unclouded Vision: all its life is spent in unceasing acts of love and worship or contrition, and of simple trust, of praise and prayer and service; *at times indeed life seems to be but one long unbroken practice of His Divine Presence.*"

If this had been written by someone who had nothing to do but preach and pray, I should not find so much in it as I do when I remember that it was said by a cook, who had to give his mind to what the foolish world calls common work.

The Lord of Brother Lawrence, who is our dear Lord too, help us to grow more and more into this life which is one unbroken practice of His blessed Presence.

❧

July 29

*Therefore shall ye abide at the door of the tabernacle of
the congregation day and night seven days, and keep the
charge of the Lord, that ye die not: for so I am commanded.
So Aaron and his sons did all things which the Lord
commanded by the hand of Moses.*
Lev. 8:35–36

"As the Lord commanded Moses": the words recur
often in these chapters. Sooner or later every child of
the Father, every servant of the heavenly Master, has to
learn that he is not here to do as he likes, but as the Lord
commands. "For so I am commanded" is Moses' single
explanation as he gives a certain duty to men who might
easily have preferred another.

Here is a beautiful word from St. Augustine's *City
of God:* "In that blessed city no one, in any lower place,
shall envy his superior; for no one will ever wish to be
that to which he has not been appointed. Together with
his reward, each shall have the gift of a great contentment, so as to desire no more than he has got. There we
shall rest and see, there we shall see and love, and there
we shall all love and praise in the City of God."

Ask for *the gift of a great contentment* in obeying
God's commands today.

July 30

And when they came to Nachon's threshing floor, Uzzah put
forth his hand to the ark of God, and took hold of it; for the
oxen shook it. And the anger of the Lord was kindled against
Uzzah, and God smote him there for his error;
and there he died by the ark of God.
2 Sam. 6:6–7

The judgment of God on what *seemed* a trivial fault
was a flashing forth of His thought about all unspiritual
service. For that is what the service of Uzzah was; and
not his only, but David's too, and that of all who set the
ark of God upon a cart. God had said that the ark was
not to be put on a cart, but it was to be carried on men's
shoulders.

The cart was a Philistine expedient (1 Sam. 6:7–8).
It has been truly said that the Church is full of Philistine
ways of doing service to Christ. But those ways are not
acceptable to God. The Uzzah story tells us so.

Let us follow His wishes in every smallest detail,
unconfused by the voices and customs around us.

July 31

*Having therefore these promises, dearly beloved, let us cleanse
ourselves from all filthiness of the flesh and spirit,
perfecting holiness in the fear of God.*
2 Cor. 7:1

I have been sent some beautiful Caladium flowers.
When this flower first opens it is hot inside (its tem-
perature has been taken, 104° F), but as it grows to perfection this excitement of heat passes. The perfect flower
is normal.

In the spiritual world, too, there can be heat and
excitement. The ferment of an old truth newly apprehended (for there is no such thing as a new truth) may
very easily cause it. The devil delights to have it so, and
it is easy to see why. If we become interested in ourselves and occupied in taking our own temperatures, so
to speak, then that truth which should bring blessing
will either slip out of sight or be put out of focus.

Our Lord said (in Luke 12:27), *Consider the lilies
how they grow;* — consider the Caladiums — *they toil
not, they spin not.* God lays His cool hand upon them
and perfects them. Think of that word in 2 Corinthians 7:1: *perfecting holiness.* There is a crisis of new
birth, then — if the Lord has His way unhindered
— a quiet growth and perfecting, which may take the
form of a series of crises. But always it is an inwardly
quiet thing.

Just before Paul wrote about perfecting holiness he wrote about common life (2 Cor. 6:3–10). Isn't this a wonderful word for us? *Giving no offence in anything, that the ministry be not blamed: but in all things approving ourselves as the ministers of God, in much patience....*

I am glad patience comes first. But read it all.

August 1

Oh how great is Thy goodness, which Thou hast laid up for them that fear Thee; which Thou hast wrought for them that trust in Thee before the sons of men!
Ps. 31:19

Is not this a simply delightful pot of manna? Delitzsch has an enlarging word on the meaning of the Hebrew noun translated *goodness*. It means the sum of good which God has treasured up for the constant and ever-increasing use and enjoyment of His saints.

For years I lost the comfort of the promises specially spoken to saints, because I knew that I was miles from being one. So I passed the blessings on to others, feeling they didn't and couldn't have anything to do with me. But one day suddenly I saw that the love of God has an amazing power, for Romans 4:17 tells us that God *calleth those things which be not as though they were*.

So let the least of us fear not, but with what Delitzsch calls "adoring admiration and triumphant certainty" worship Him, saying, "Oh how great is Thy goodness, and how great is Thy beauty. How eternal Thy love, O my Lord and my God."

❧

August 2

And to the office of Eleazar the son of Aaron the priest
pertaineth . . . the oversight of all the tabernacle, and of all that
therein is, in the sanctuary, and in the vessels thereof.
Num. 4:16

In the day when I cried Thou answeredst me,
and strengthenedst me with strength in my soul.
Ps. 138:3

Numbers 4 is one of the many chapters in the Bible which hallows detail. "The oversight of the tabernacle *and of all that therein is"* included such detail as the naming of the separate instruments used. There is something very loving in the way burden-bearing is recognized as part of service — Aaron and his sons were to *appoint them every one to his service and to his burden* (Num. 4:19). The God with whom we have to do is a God who understands.

Are you burdened in your service today because of the continual necessity of looking after details? In work of every sort there are a thousand tiny things which do not seem to matter, and yet matter very much. Indeed there is nothing, except things concerning our own comfort or desires, about which we can say "It doesn't matter."

How can our spirit be kept fresh and sweet and buoyant and tireless? A quick look up, "O Lord, Thou knowest," will restore us. *In the day* — in the moment — *when I cried Thou answeredst me, and strengthenedst me with strength in my soul.*

241

August 3

Forasmuch then as Christ hath suffered for us in the flesh, arm yourselves likewise with the same mind.
1 Pet. 4:1

When Peter wrote that, he must have remembered the hour when he was not armed with his Lord's brave and patient mind. He did not refer to his fall. He never did refer to it so far as we know, yet the memory and the pain of it seem to underlie all his writings.

There is no such thing for a child of God as a lost pain, not even the pain of sin. Our discouragements and failures, even our sins (because of what they teach us of the precious blood of Christ) can be turned to help for others.

Many, O Lord my God, are Thy wonderful works which Thou hast done, and Thy thoughts which are to us-ward (Ps. 40:5). Who but our blessed Lord Jesus could have had such a thought as this? Who but He would have said about the poor broken fragments of our lives, *Gather up the fragments . . . that nothing be lost* (John 6:12)? O Lord, our dear Lord, "There is no one like Thee."

August 4

*And he said unto him, Son, thou art ever with me,
and all that I have is thine.
Luke 15:31*

Such words need no words to explain them. They
pass explanation. Only the Spirit of God can open them
to us. But this from Ter Steegen may help us to understand them a little:

"Hath not each heart a passion and a dream?
  Each some companionship for ever sweet?
And each in saddest skies some silver gleam,
  And each some passing joy, too fair and fleet?
And each a staff and stay, though frail it prove,
  And each a face he fain would ever see?
And what have I? An endless Heaven of love,
  A rapture, and a glory, and a calm;
A life that is an everlasting psalm,
  All, O Beloved, in Thee."

*Son, thou art ever with Me, and all that I have is
thine.* Father, I would be ever with Thee, and all that I
have is Thine.

August 5

Many, O Lord my God, are Thy wonderful works which
Thou hast done, and Thy thoughts which are to us-ward:
they cannot be reckoned up in order unto Thee:
if I would declare and speak of them,
they are more than can be numbered.
Ps. 40:5

My room is on the pathway, and often as someone passes by he glances in and smiles. That smile has lightened the minutes, for me, for a long time afterwards.

Through this very little thing I have learned afresh how much our Heavenly Father cares for a loving thought — a thought that is like a smile.

My thoughts of those who passed my window were many. But they knew very little, if anything, of them. Our Father's thoughts to us-ward are many. We only know a few of them, but they are flowing us-ward all the time.

I wonder whether He watches for a thought from us, just as I have watched for a smile through the window? Don't let us forget, as we go here and there, that there is One who cares very much for these little, quick upward glances that tell Him we are loving Him. How good it is, to know that He cares so much for the thought that is like a smile.

&

August 6

The beast of the field shall honor Me, the dragons and the
owls: because I give waters in the wilderness, and rivers in
the desert, to give drink to My people, My chosen.
Isa. 43:20

And they thirsted not when He led them through the deserts:
He caused the waters to flow out of the rock for them:
He clave the rock also, and the waters gushed out.
Isa. 48:21

Did you ever wake up in the morning feeling like
an owl? If any prefer the other reading, ostrich (Isa.
43:20 margin), it comes to the same in the end. The ostrich is not, in Scripture, an illustration of intelligence.
(Job 39:13–17 settles that.) But it is these very birds
that "honor Me because I give waters in the wilderness,
and rivers in the desert."

There are days when every ostrich and owl among
us will have the chance to do that, for there are bound to
be dry, desert days. Don't let us miss the chance. There
will be no dryness in the Country whither we are hasten-
ing. Here, only here, is the opportunity to drink of the
waters in the wilderness and to lead others to the rivers.

Let us witness to the truth of such words as Isaiah
51:3: *For the Lord shall comfort Zion: He will comfort*
all her waste places; and He will make her wilderness like
Eden, and her desert like the garden of the Lord; joy and
gladness shall be found therein, thanksgiving and the voice
of melody.

August 7

His great love wherewith He loved us,
even when we were dead in sins.
Eph. 2:4–5

He loved us even when we were dead.

There is a Tamil poem which compares the love of the birds which fly away when the lake dries up with the love of the flowers which cleave to it even to the withering of death. It is a picture of the love of the One who loved us even when we were dead, and for love of us gave Himself to the withering of death.

"Are we eternal to one another?" asks the Tamil proverb, and it expects a sad negative. Instead we can sing out an answer of triumph, for in eternal love we are eternal to one another. Love is immortal: Calvary leads to Easter Day.

August 8

Ought not Christ to have suffered these things,
and to enter into His glory?
Luke 24:26

And He began to teach them, that the Son of Man must
suffer many things, and be rejected . . . and be killed,
and after three days rise again.
Mark 8:31

"There is in God — some say —
   A deep but dazzling darkness; as men here
Say it is late and dusky, because they
   See not all clear."

The eternal *Must,* the eternal *Ought not?* of suffering is a deep but dazzling darkness. It is inescapable in
the life of all who would follow the Crucified.

It is true that we do not "see all clear." But we do
understand a little of what our Lord meant when He
said, *Ought not Christ to have suffered?* And so we come
to understand that suffering is not something we should
pray to escape, or pray that others whom we love should
escape.

"It was the way the Master went;
   Should not the servant tread it still?"

August 9

He was known of them in breaking of bread.
Luke 24:35

"O man likeminded, who in companionship with me sweetened our food" (Ps. 55:13–14 Septuagint). That word was written in grief, of Judas who betrayed his trust. But could any words show more happily what the companionship of our Lord and Master does for us at meal times, when we do not forget to meet Him there?

Lord, Thou hast heard the desire of the humble: Thou wilt prepare their heart, Thou wilt cause Thine ear to hear (Ps. 10:17). Our dear Lord hears our desire and He prepares our heart. Then we are ready to meet others, and together we meet Him and know Him in the breaking of bread as we eat together.

It is well to give time to the preparation of the mind. Push away thoughts of disturbing things. Recall happy things, and share these things. Meal times are not times for discussion of problems and difficulties; banish these wearinesses. If all pool their treasures, tiny little treasures of fun, then the devil who is greatly interested in the meal times of Christians won't have a chance.

Isn't it a good thing to begin to practice for the Marriage Supper of the Lamb (Rev. 19:9)?

August 10

Let us therefore fear, lest, a promise being left us of entering into His rest, any of you should seem to come short of it.
Heb. 4:1

As we journey on there will be rivers, and we shall find neither bridges nor boats nor airplanes. But the rivers can be leaped by a spring of the will — the resolute will *not* to come short of the promise of entering into His rest. There will be Giants' Valleys, and mountains of immense and impossible obstacles. But nothing can hold up one who follows a Conqueror.

The devil continually tries to keep us on the near side of our rivers, and to entangle us in valley and mountain, till we forget that we are here to overcome, not to be overcome. All this is part of the intended discipline of life.

Two more Tamil proverbs are: "If one *will,* what is impossible?" and "If there be love, even the impossible becomes possible." God give us the will to conquer, the will that refuses defeat. Defeat need never be, for all the time "He goes before." So it will be till, as it were, He turns in the road and we see His face and are satisfied. For *I shall be satisfied by a vision of Thee* (Ps. 17:15 Rotherham). That is the blessed end of our journey.

August 11

Come unto Me, all ye that labor and are heavy laden, and I
will give you rest. Take My yoke upon you, and learn of Me;
for I am meek and lowly in heart:
and ye shall find rest unto your souls.
Matt. 11:28–29

Young gives the meaning of *rest* as "rest again, cease from, rest thoroughly." *Rest again* is the word for today. We are not promised smooth roads, but rough. When things are smooth we should look up in delight and thanksgiving, thinking of them as breathing spaces rather than as the normal condition of things. Rough roads make it certain that we shall often come to our Lord for rest.

Our dear Lord will never be surprised by our frequent coming. He will never tire of resting us, and in the rest He gives His strength. His invitation stands sure: *Come unto Me and I will give you rest,* rest again.

August 12

Thou, O Lord God, art the thing that I long for.
Ps. 71:4 (BCP)

. . . He hath longed for her.
Ps. 132:14 (BCP)

It is not strange that we should long for our Lord. How could we help it? But it is surely the wonder of all wonders that He should long for us.

For the Lord hath chosen Zion to be an habitation for Himself: He hath longed for her. Zion, poor fallen sinful Zion; man, poor fallen sinful man; *me* (how fallen, how sinful, only He who knows all knows), *He hath longed for me.*

Lord Jesus, help me to meet longing with longing, love with love. Thou, O Lord, art the Thing that I long for. *I will love Thee, O Lord, my strength* (Ps. 18:1).

August 13

And whatsoever we ask, we receive of Him, because we keep
His commandments, and do those things that are pleasing
in His sight. And this is His commandment, That we should
believe on the name of His Son Jesus Christ,
and love one another, as He gave us commandment.
1 John 3:22–23

United prayer is perhaps the most infallible ther-
mometer we possess for detecting the slightest deviation
from the normal. The normal is the clear peace of hearts
perfectly tuned to one another because perfectly tuned
to love. When that is so, then prayer is a harmony. The
notes make chords, the silences are as rests in music.
There is the Selah in both its senses, Pause and Praise.
In such meetings there is a most wonderful uplifting, as
adoration passes into intercession. Such prayer is worth
the time it costs for preparation.

Let us prepare for prayer. Is there any inward
thought not wholly Christ-like about some trouble-
some, disappointing, ungrateful other soul? Is there any
self-centred thought which blinds my heart to others'
needs?

If so, God help us to face it before we meet to pray.
A long look at Calvary shames the soul as nothing else
does, and unites it too with fellow Christians, for it ban-
ishes the littleness that can divide. It shames it out of us.

August 14

He shall choose our inheritance for us,
the excellency of Jacob whom He loved.
Ps. 47:4

Have you ever looked longingly at another life and wished that you had as much as it has to offer? But *He shall choose,* and He does not call the inheritance of any Jacob "poor." He calls it the *excellency* of Jacob. The marvel is not that we have so little to offer, but that we have anything at all. There was no worthiness in Jacob. *Whom He loved* is the only explanation.

But — and is not this comforting? — God needs each separate soul, each personality with the inheritance of His choice, for the perfecting of His purpose in the spiritual creation. And when it is perfected He will be satisfied, and we too shall be satisfied, "lost in wonder, love and praise" that we ever were allowed the smallest share in it.

August 15

The Lord is my firm support.
Ps. 18:2 (Septuagint)

Samuel Rutherford knew God as his firm support. In 1637 he wrote in one of his letters: "I know that no man hath a velvet cross, but that the cross is made of that which God will have it."

Another of his words which can encourage us today is: "When I lose breath climbing up the mountain, He maketh new breath."

What a firm support our Lord is, to even the weakest of His children!

August 16

*But when they saw Him walking upon the sea, they supposed
it had been a spirit, and cried out: for they all saw Him,
and were troubled. And immediately He talked with them,
and saith unto them, Be of good cheer: it is I; be not afraid.*
Mark 6:49–50

Have you ever had a good time with your Lord and
then afterwards been tempted to wonder if it was really
all you had believed it was? Was it truly a divine touch
that you felt on your spirit? Was it truly His very own
voice that you heard? Or was it just a feeling, imagination, not true?

The Aramaic of Mark 6:49 is, "They thought it was
a *false* vision.... And immediately He spoke to them,
and said, Have courage, it is I; do not be afraid."

It will be for us as it was for those troubled men.
In moments of temptation, when we doubt and fear
about the reality of our experience, He will speak with
us. He will say, "Have courage. It is I. It was I: it was no
false vision. Do not be afraid." And then we shall go on
to prove His presence in the common life of common
days.

August 17

And this is the confidence that we have in Him, that, if we ask
any thing according to His will, He heareth us: and if we know
that He hear us, whatsoever we ask, we know that
we have the petitions that we desired of Him.
1 John 5:14–15

There is great comfort in one of the glorious prayers
of the New Testament. No one knows who wrote it, but
we do know that it is an inspired prayer, and so there
can be no doubt whatever about its being answered. It
is one of the prayers that fit the conditions of 1 John
5:14–15.

It is Hebrews 13:20–21. Weymouth translates it:
Now may God who gives peace, and brought Jesus, our
Lord, up again from among the dead — even Him who,
by virtue of the blood of the eternal Covenant, is the great
Shepherd of the sheep — fully equip you with every grace
that you may need for the doing of His will, producing in
us that which will truly please Him through Jesus Christ.
To Him be the glory to the ages of the ages! Amen.

The Lord strengthen us to take hold upon these
words for whatever is the need of the day. He is faithful.
He has not given us up because we have so often disappointed Him. Let us trust and not be afraid.

August 18

For since the beginning of the world men have not heard, nor perceived by the ear, neither hath the eye seen, O God, beside Thee, what He hath prepared for him that waiteth for Him. Thou meetest him that rejoiceth and worketh righteousness, those that remember Thee in Thy ways.
Isa. 64:4–5

There is none that calleth upon Thy name, that stirreth up himself to take hold of Thee.
Isa. 64:7

There is such a thing as a shining contentment with the will of God. Any lack there is a loss to prayer. *Thou meetest him that rejoiceth* comes just before the word that so often impels us to take time for prayer, *There is none that stirreth up himself to take hold of Thee.* Before the assurance that He will indeed meet him who rejoices, comes the glorious word that is like a burst of sunshine: "For since the beginning of the world men have not heard or perceived or seen *what He hath prepared for him that waiteth for Him.*"

August 19

*I will mention the loving kindnesses of the Lord, and the
praises of the Lord, according to all that the Lord hath
bestowed on us, and the great goodness toward the house of
Israel, which He hath bestowed on them according to His
mercies, and according to the multitude of
His lovingkindnesses.*
Isa. 63:7

All kinds of things are reminders of the lovingkindness of the Lord. Friends, letters, flowers, pictures, all these and many more speak of the wonderful lovingkindness of our God to us who are unworthy of even one of His good gifts. As we think of all His love has already given us, and of the multitude of His lovingkindnesses which we have experienced, our prayer becomes glad and grateful and full of thanksgiving. Prayer starts from a place of joy and confidence.

But sometimes we are tempted to discouragement. So often we have believed that what we asked was about to be given, and then have been disappointed. But delays are for the trial of faith, not for its discouragement. Often we have had to wait for years for our best and dearest gifts. When they came we looked up to our Lord in adoration, "Lord, this was worth waiting for." So it will be again. He has done so much for us. Will He not also do this that we ask Him today?

August 20

Our soul waits on for the Lord.
Ps. 33:20 (Kay)

Is it not comforting and strengthening to faith to take hold of these words? *Our soul waits on for the Lord.* Kay's note is: "Man's reliance on God being the only — but all-prevailing — claim he has on God's help."

The Lord is *our* help and *our* shield, just as He was David's. If only we wait on, in unshaken trust, *our heart shall rejoice in Him, because we have trusted in His holy name* (v. 21).

August 21

And this I pray, that your love may abound yet more and more in knowledge and in all judgment.
Phil. 1:9

That is a generous word — *abound.* God uses generous words.

The love for which Paul prays is a wonderful kind of love. It does not love in a merely earthly way or in a weak way. Does my friendship with that friend of mine help towards unselfishness? Does it draw others in or does it push them out? Is it discerning — wise in understanding how best to help? Does it always put Christ and others first?

Abounding love of this sort is our great need. Such love is always looking out for chances to do loving things. It runs the second mile as a matter of course, for it is continually doing more than it need.

Let us pray that this love may abound more and more in us. God is love, and we can never draw too much upon Him. That sea will never run dry.

❧

August 22

That ye may approve things that are excellent; that ye may be sincere and without offence till the day of Christ.
Phil. 1:10

"So that you may test the things that differ" is Bishop Moule's version in his *Philippian Studies*.

Almost the first thing a baby learns to do is to test things that differ. Put a new thing in a baby's hand and watch it. It turns it round, looks at it, tries to bite it. Once when I was small I put a piece of soap in my mouth thinking it was butter. I never did that again.

Paul prayed that the people of Philippi might approve the things that are excellent — not go on eating soap when they found it was not butter. What about us? Do we test and approve the excellent? That means, are we doing every single thing, great and small, seen and unseen, as unto the Lord?

❧

August 23

If any man come to Me, and hate not his father, and mother, and wife, and children, and brethren, and sisters, yea, and his own life also, he cannot be My disciple.
Luke 14:26

If any man come to Me, and hate not. . . . That is the point that halts us. We must remember that here we have the Oriental idiom of sharp contrasts, and the word hate is used as the opposite of love. Our Lord was not claiming that we should have a malicious attitude of heart towards our loved ones in order to be His disciples. He was facing the possibility of competition in loyalty with the things that He names.

He did not name a low thing, an ignoble thing. He was facing the possibility, which often occurs, of a conflict between that which is beautiful in itself and loyalty to Him. Nothing is fairer, finer, more beautiful in human life than love of father, and mother, and wife, and children, and brothers and sisters. Yet these fair things may, and often do, challenge our loyalty to our Lord.

Thus He was declaring that, if ever an hour strikes when there is a conflict between the call of the highest earthly love and the call of Christ, then there is only one thing to be done. We must trample across our own hearts and go after Him, without any compromise and any questionings.

August 24

*And whosoever doth not bear his cross, and come after Me,
cannot be My disciple.*
Luke 14:27

The taking up of the cross always means the emptying of the life of everything that is merely selfish in motive, and high things may become that. If there shall come a moment when a man has to choose between the call of Christ to sacrificial life and service, and the appeal of high and beautiful earthly affection, there is only one thing to be done according to these terms of Jesus. That is to follow Him.

He calls for much; He calls for everything. He calls for the march that may have no return and can have no compromise. He demands this loyalty because His enterprise is a crusade. Its method is that of the cross, and there is no other way. Because He goes that way, His disciple also must go that way.

❧

August 25

Let this mind be in you, which was also in Christ Jesus:
who, being in the form of God, thought it not robbery to be
equal with God: but made Himself of no reputation, and
took upon Him the form of a servant, and was made in the
likeness of men: and being found in fashion as a man, He
humbled Himself, and became obedient unto death,
even the death of the cross.
Phil. 2:5–8:

We never touch the realm of the cross until we are
suffering vicariously, until our suffering is the suffering of sympathy with others, and our strength is being
poured out in order to help others. That is the cross. We
can only interpret the cross by His cross.

It is an arresting and revealing thing to take the demands of Jesus as uttered at Caesarea Philippi and place
them side by side with the greatest thing written under
inspiration by the apostle concerning the Lord Himself.
Read what Paul wrote in Philippians 2:5–8.

There is the cross. *He emptied Himself. The death of
the cross.*

If I am going after Him I must deny myself. He went
all the way to the cross. If I am going to be His disciple I
must accept that cross as the principle of all life and service.
That is what He meant here. He says: "If men are coming after Me, they must go My way." Discipleship does not
merely mean the salvation of the soul. It means fellowship
with Him in the travail, and then the triumph. Unless we
are prepared for that, He says we cannot be His disciples.

August 26

And the king's servants said unto the king, Behold, thy
servants are ready to do whatsoever
my lord the king shall appoint.
2 Sam. 15:15

Any-thing
Any-where
Any-how
Any-when.
Are we truly ready for this today?

August 27

I know whom I have believed.
2 Tim. 1:12

I will trust and not be afraid.
Isa. 12:2

And Abraham said unto his young men...I and the lad will
go yonder and worship, and come again to you.
Gen. 22:5

Accounting that God was able to raise him up,
even from the dead.
Heb. 11:19

I know whom I have believed. I will trust and not be afraid. I know...I will. It is good to use difficult circumstances to prove the peace-giving power of these words.

This is what Abraham did when he calmly told his young men to stay with the ass, and that he *and Isaac* would return. God had said years before to Abraham, *"In Isaac shall thy seed be called"* (Gen. 21:12). He must have held fast to that promise for he was certain that something beyond human belief and experience would happen if necessary. He believed that God was able even to raise Isaac from the dead. So he must have said to himself as he walked up the hillside: "I know whom I have believed.... I will trust and not be afraid." I know: I will.

The end of that glorious *I know* verse is strength

and peace and comfort. For all to whom has been committed the care of souls, they are golden words that lead straight to the peace of God. *I am persuaded that He is able to keep that which I have committed unto Him,* or as the RV margin says, *that which He hath committed unto me* (2 Tim. 1:12).

He is able. I know. I will trust.

August 28

He knoweth our frame; He remembereth that we are dust.
Ps. 103:14

He knoweth the way that I take: when He hath tried me,
I shall come forth as gold.
Job 23:10

Perhaps those words, *He knoweth*, are meant for you today because God has allowed you some special trial of faith. The love of God is very brave. He does not hold trial off lest we should be overwhelmed. He lets it come and then gloriously strengthens us to meet it. And at the end, *I shall come forth as gold.*

August 29

But there [Jerusalem] the glorious Lord will be unto us a place of broad rivers and streams; wherein shall go no galley with oars, neither shall gallant ship pass thereby.
Isa. 33:21

Circumstances are nothing to God. There is no river near Jerusalem, that city of continual unrest. But He speaks of Jerusalem as of a peaceful city on a river, and a great river too, up which the ships of the enemy could sail — but they never shall.

God teaches us as we teach our little children. He uses pictures. This picture meant to the men who first saw it that the ships of the nations whom they greatly feared would never have power to sail up to their city. God's spiritual Zion would be protected from her enemies.

Jerusalem the city of turmoil, a quiet habitation. Is your heart quiet? God can quiet it. Jerusalem the riverless city, glad and safe because of its glorious Lord, who is to it a place of broad rivers and streams — what a word for us for today!

August 30

They went, and entered into a village of the Samaritans, to make ready for Him. And they did not receive Him, because His face was as though He would go to Jerusalem.
Luke 9:52–53

But a certain Samaritan, as he journeyed, came where he was: and when he saw him, he had compassion on him.
Luke 10:33

Of all unkind things, one of the unkindest is to refuse to give a tired traveler a place to rest. No Indian would do that. But the Samaritans did it: *They did not receive Him.*

When anyone has been unkind to us, what do we feel inclined to do? How do we feel inclined to speak of them?

A little while after this unkindness of the Samaritans, our Lord Jesus told a story about kindness, and of all the people of Palestine He chose a Samaritan as an illustration of true, tender kindness.

If we meet unkindness today, let us react as our dear Lord did.

August 31

After that He appeared in another form.
Mark 16:12

And in that day ye shall ask Me nothing.
John 16:23

We always expect the Lord to come to us in a joy. Instead of that He sometimes appears in another form, He comes in a big disappointment.

In the day that we see Him all will be clear. The mysteries which now perplex us will be illuminated. One day we shall see the glory to our glorious God and the good to all of us contained in the disappointment we cannot understand.

So let us live as those who believe this to be true. Let us praise before we see. Let us thank our Lord for trusting us to trust Him.

September 1

Over the camels also was Obil the Ishmaelite.
1 Chron. 27:30

Have you to try to help people who are rather like camels? You want them to go one way, and they go another. You try persuasion and they turn sulky. It is difficult to be patient with an animal that never looks pleased. It is very difficult to be patient with human camels.

But God knows all about you and your difficulties, and your name is not forgotten by Him. He thought the name of a camel driver who lived three thousand years ago worth writing in His Book. The names of thousands of great kings are buried and forgotten, but the name of David's camel driver is remembered to this day: *Over the camels was Obil.*

Obil means "driver" or "leader." I expect he sometimes found leading better than driving, and so sometimes shall we. God give His Obils patience to deal with their camels.

❧

September 2

And over the asses was Jehdeiah the Meronothite.
1 Chron. 27:30

Jehdeiah's name meant "Union of Jah." I once had a letter from a man who was trying to run a big political organization in India. He said he had sympathy with Paul, who wrote in 1 Corinthians 15:32 that he had fought with wild beasts at Ephesus, but he was quite sure it was still harder to fight with asses.

I am glad that we do not have to fight with asses, but we certainly have to look after them sometimes. I wonder if Jehdeiah found comfort in his name? Work like his needs patience, firmness, kindness, and these good things are not naturally in us. John 15:5, *WITHOUT Me ye can do nothing,* is a word all who have to do with asses understand. But *WITH Me* — that is the secret. God in us can be patient and kind, even with poor asses.

God make all of us who have to do with asses His Jehdeiahs.

September 3

And over the flocks was Jaziz the Hagerite.
1 Chron. 27:31

His name meant "Shining." Most of us have sometimes to do with camels, sometimes with asses, but oftenest, thank God, with the flocks of the Good Shepherd.

There was once an unhappy shepherd, Zechariah, who dismissed three under-shepherds in one month, and said, *And my soul loathed them, and their soul also abhorred me* (Zech. 11:8). We have a very different flock from that committed to poor Zechariah, and quite different fellow-shepherds. Are we half grateful enough for the joys of good fellowship?

Jaziz had a beautiful name — *Shining*. No dullness, no heavy-heartedness as he tended the flocks. God make us all to be Jazizes — happy shepherds, shining shepherds.

❧

September 4

Beautiful art thou, My fair one, majestic as bannered hosts.
Song of Sol. 6:4 (Rotherham)

Just now a tree on the very top of the hill is all tipped with the crimson of young leaves. Through the field glasses it is like an army with banners, and every single little crimson banner is held out and waves in the wind.

Beautiful art thou, My fair one, majestic as bannered hosts. That is what our Lord calls us, thinking of us as so much better than we really are, for that is His loving custom. If we truly love Him it is impossible to hear such words without wanting to rise to them.

Are we like an army with banners? Or are we slouching along anyhow? It would spoil a bannered host if a single banner-bearer trailed his banner in the dust, and marched out of step, and slacked. Don't let any one of us think, "It doesn't matter about me." It *does* matter about you.

❧

September 5

Thou hast given a banner to them that fear Thee,
that it may be displayed because of the truth.
Ps. 60:4

God does not give us our banners to hide away out of sight, but to display. A banner is the sign of our allegiance; it shows what side we are on in a fight. It is like the colors we wear when we are playing in athletic games.

When the devil tries to get you to behave as a Christian should not, show your banners — show your colors. "I am Christ's. I can't do that."

The wonderful thing is, that the moment we show our colors the Captain is by our side, and from Him (not from us) the devil flees. James 4:7 says, *Resist the devil, and he will flee from you,* for he sees behind you the mighty Conqueror who won on Calvary.

September 6

Neither do men light a candle, and put it under a bushel,
but on a candlestick; and it giveth light unto all
that are in the house.
Matt. 5:15

"The night has a thousand eyes,
    And the day but one;
Yet the light of the bright world dies
    With dying sun.

The mind has a thousand eyes
    And the heart but one;
Yet the light of the whole life dies
    When love is done."

I do not know who wrote this little poem, but it is true.

Do you feel you can't do much for anyone? I feel like that often. But we can love. And love is like light. If the candle of love is shining, then even though it is only a little candle it gives light to all who are in the house.

God make us all His candles.

❧

September 7

And when He had looked round about on them with anger, being grieved for the hardness of their hearts, He saith unto the man, Stretch forth thine hand. And he stretched it out: and his hand was restored whole as the other.
Mark 3:5

And when His friends heard of it... they said, He is beside Himself. And the scribes which came down from Jerusalem said, He hath Beelzebub, and by the prince of the devils casteth He out devils. And He called them unto Him, and said unto them in parables, How can Satan cast out Satan?
Mark 3:21–23

When our Lord had looked round on them with anger, being grieved for their hardness of heart, He said a loving word to a poor man who was probably a good deal troubled because of the excitement in the place.

What do we say when we are grieved and angry? Do we speak a kind word to someone who needs it?

Some said: "He is beside Himself." Others declared: "He casts out devils by the prince of the devils." But He asked, *How can Satan cast out Satan?* There was not a word of indignant self-defense, just a quiet question. It was the overflow of the sweetness and peace of His heart. When we are unkindly and unjustly accused, perhaps just when we have been helping someone, how do we react? Perhaps there is not time for a long prayer in that moment of quick temptation, but there is always time for a look up to Him. "Thy sweetness, Lord. Thy peace, Lord."

It will always be given.

September 8

*And He commanded them to make all sit down by companies
upon the green grass.*
Mark 6:39

He maketh me to lie down in green pastures.
Psalm 23:2

Those who do most in the day and who always have
time for one thing more are those who know what it
is to sit down on the green grass. It is not the bustling,
chattery people who do most for others. It is those who
know most of quietness.

Before our Lord Jesus could feed the people, He had
to make them sit down. Before He can feed us we too
must sit down. David sat before the Lord; he was quiet
before his God. Even if we have not a long time to spend
in the morning with our God, much can be received in a
very few minutes if only we are quiet. Sometimes it takes
a little while to gather our scattered thoughts and quiet
our soul. Even so, don't hurry; make it sit down on the
green grass.

Gather my thoughts, good Lord, they fitful roam,
Like children bent on foolish wandering,
Or vanity of fruitless wayfaring;
    O call them home.

❧

September 9

*And His disciples answered Him, From whence can a man
satisfy these men with bread here in the wilderness?*
Mark 8:4

The disciples needed faith that day. They had to
persuade the people that it was worth their while to sit
down, and this before they saw how they would be fed.
A hungry, disappointed Eastern crowd can be difficult
to handle. Suppose, after sitting down in expectation,
that crowd had found itself deceived? That fear must
have come to the disciples.

As they brought their poor little loaves and fishes,
the disciples, who were at that time far from what they
afterwards became, must have been tempted to wonder
whether what they had seen happen before would really
happen again.

We are tempted like that. We need to have faith that
the soul we are trying to persuade to sit down, so that its
Lord may feed it, really will sit down, and really will be
fed. If there be the least doubt in our own hearts, that
doubt will somehow affect that soul. Even as we bring all
we have to offer to our Lord for His multiplying touch
and blessing, we may be assaulted by doubt. Will it be of
any use? Will anything happen? Or will it be all in vain?

The answer to such questions is found in words like
this: *Your labor is not in vain in the Lord. God hath not
given us the spirit of fear. Experience [worketh] hope* (1
Cor. 15:58; 2 Tim. 1:7; Rom. 5:4).

September 10

The feeding of five thousand with five loaves and two fishes.
Mark 6:35–44

The feeding of four thousand with seven loaves
and a few small fishes.
Mark 8:1–9

Some hearts are often troubled by the fear of failing those who look to them for help. They realize their own lack of everything which is required, and sometimes become more than a little discouraged and fearful. "Sooner or later," they feel, "someone will come to me for what I cannot give, and go away disappointed."

There are words in the two stories of the feeding of the two multitudes which can help. *"Shall we go and buy?" "How many loaves have ye? Go and see."* And when He had taken the five loaves and two fishes, He looked up to heaven, and blessed, and brake the loaves, and gave them to His disciples, and the two fishes He divided. *And they did all eat, and were filled. And they took up twelve baskets full of the fragments, and of the fishes.*

Then on the second occasion, *"From whence can a man satisfy these men?" "How many loaves have ye?"* And He took their seven loaves, and gave thanks, and brake, and gave; and also a few small fishes. *So they did eat, and were filled: and they took up of . . . that was left seven baskets.*

Five loaves or seven, two fishes or a few, nothing was

sufficient to meet the need. All was as little as this that *we* have to offer now. But if only we give all we have, just as it is in its littleness, into His hands to be dealt with as He wills, it will be multiplied. It will be enough for all He wants to do with it, and more than enough.

Let us give all we have to give, to be blessed and broken in His hands.

September 11

*There were thunders and lightnings, and a thick cloud upon
the mount, and the voice of the trumpet exceeding loud; so
that all the people that was in the camp trembled. And when
the voice of the trumpet sounded long, and waxed louder and
louder, Moses spake, and God answered him by a voice.*
Exod. 19:16, 19

*And there was a cloud that overshadowed them and a voice
came out of the cloud saying, This is My beloved Son: hear Him.*
Mark 9:7

After the wonder of the feeding of the multitudes,
and the walk on the sea, and the healing of many — after all these marvels *there was a cloud that overshadowed
them;* and they feared as they entered into the cloud.

It is often like that: it was so with Moses. First in
his experience came the bush that was not consumed,
and the amazing doing of his God in Egypt, and by the
Red Sea, and in the wilderness. Then came *a thick cloud
upon the mount.*

But with Moses in that thick cloud was his God,
and Moses spoke and God answered him by a voice.
Peter also spoke, and a voice came out of the cloud. It
is always so; in the cloud is a Presence and a Voice. The
Voice says to us, *This is My beloved Son: hear Him.* THIS
that has come upon you like a cloud, THIS is the Presence of My beloved Son and your beloved Savior; hear
Him. And when we listen we hear Him say, "It is I" —
(this "it" is I) — "be not afraid."

September 12

*Then Peter began to say unto Him, Lo, we have left all, and
have followed Thee. And Jesus answered and said, Verily
I say unto you, There is no man that hath left house, or
brethren, or sisters, or father, or mother, or wife, or children,
or lands, for My sake, and the gospel's, but he shall receive
an hundredfold now in this time . . . with persecutions;
and in the world to come eternal life.*
Mark 10:28–30

"Leave all and thou shalt find all." This is a word
for each one of us, for as the same old book says, "This
is not one day's work nor children's play." It is not a
little matter to leave all — all of self, its desires, pride
and ways. But if we do we shall find all that our Lord
has to give us.

Do we want to live this life? Are we in earnest about
it? Or do we still want to hold on to the wretched rags
of self and self-pleasing? God can deliver us from these,
and strengthen us in very truth to leave all, that we may
find all.

September 13

They were sore afraid. And there was a cloud that
overshadowed them.... And suddenly, when they had looked
round about, they saw no man any more,
save Jesus only with themselves.
Mark 9:6–8

Great books have been written to buttress faith in
the truth of the Bible, but the ultimate proof is that this
Book of books finds us where we are, meets our deepest
needs, and speaks to us with a voice utterly different
from any other voice.

Here, for example, something is told us that is
spirit and life to the heart of a Christian who is in the
shadow of a cloud. That heart knows how alone it feels
then. Yes, but not alone, for it is then that it experiences
as never before "Jesus only with myself."

Are you in trouble about something? Take this
word as you would a flower in your hand. You cannot
see the fragrance of a flower, and you cannot see the
presence of your Lord, but you can let its sweetness refresh you. Look up to Him and say "Thank You" to your
Lord Jesus who is always with you.

September 14

Thy words were found, and I did eat them; and Thy word was unto me the joy and rejoicing of mine heart: for I am called by Thy name, O Lord God of hosts.
Jer. 15:16

"It's a very odd thing,
  As odd as can be,
  That whatever she eats
  Turns into Miss T."

This nice little nursery rhyme says something important. If we hastily read God's word, without taking the time or trouble to absorb it, we do not gain much. But if we take it into ourselves (Thy word was found and I did eat it), then it becomes part of us. It "turns into Miss T."

Let us take some words of His today, perhaps some simple well-known word, and do just what Miss T did with what was on her plate.

September 15

Our Lord's temptation in the wilderness.
Luke 4:1–13

"Every weapon by sharpening becomes sharp," says the Tamil proverb. How can we sharpen our sword? In one sense we cannot and need not, for the Sword of the Spirit which is the word of God never grows blunt. But we can immensely sharpen our powers of using it.

During the temptation in the wilderness our Lord met the tempter with exactly the right word. We sometimes forget that this showed He had read the book of Deuteronomy so carefully that He knew it from end to end. He knew just what room in the armory held the exact weapon He wanted. As He had no Bible with Him in the wilderness, it is certain that He knew those words by heart. The word He had read had become a part of Himself.

Do you remember Miss T?

❧

September 16

For the builders, every one had his sword girded by his side,
and so builded.
Neh. 4:18

An evangelist came for a week's work. "Please will you lend me a Bible?" he asked.

"Haven't you brought your own?"

"No, I thought I could borrow one."

Compare that with Nehemiah's builders. *Every one had his sword girded by his side.* It must have been rather in the way, dangling from his sash or belt, but he knew better than to go to work without his sword.

Our sword, of course, is a spiritual thing; it is the word of God, as Ephesians 6:17 tells us. Let us never go anywhere without it. Whatever we don't take, let us take that.

Now for today, and the foes of today, here is a great word: Psalm 144:1. *Blessed be the Lord my Strength, which teacheth my hands to war, and my fingers to fight.*

He will teach us how to use our sword today.

September 17

But Jesus answered them, My Father
worketh hitherto, and I work.
John 5:17

And they went forth, and preached everywhere,
the Lord working with them.
Mark 16:20

Some imagine God our Father is eternally resting, "doing nothing," as a child would express it. When I was small I thought of Him as forever sitting on a white throne with a blaze of light all around. A circle of people dressed in white, eternally playing harps, were always sitting just on the edge of the blaze, for a hymn said that heaven was a place where "congregations ne'er break up and Sabbaths never end." It was such an awful prospect that I had no wish to go there.

Our Lord's description of His Father was entirely different. *My Father worketh hitherto, and I work.* When later on His servants preached His word, our Lord worked with them even though He was not with them in the flesh.

What a glorious life is ours! Our Lord does not merely watch us work today, but He actually works with us.

September 18

Beloved, let us love one another: for love is of God; and everyone that loveth is born of God, and knoweth God.
1 John 4:7

Thy word have I hid in mine heart, that I might not sin against Thee.
Ps. 119:11

Beloved, let us love. Is this word so hidden in our heart that it is impossible for us to sin against our God whose name is Love?

It should be quite impossible even to think an unkind thought about another. To misjudge, or to put the worst interpretation on what someone has said or done, should be utterly impossible. If this great word, *Beloved, let us love,* is hidden in our heart it will prevent unkindness of any sort from slipping in. Sometimes, of course, we *have* to speak of wrong things, but if we can speak of wrong in another without pain — *that* is unlove.

September 19

Today if ye will hear His voice, harden not your hearts.
Heb. 4:7

Once a man wrote in a book the experiences he had had with the Lord, and the blessings he had received. When he was downhearted, he read it. But the rats, fond of eating paper, found it. One day he sent his servant for the book, and his servant returned and said: "O Master, the rats have eaten up all your experiences!"

It would be a good thing if some kind rat would eat up all our experiences if we are in the least living on them. The word is always *TODAY if ye will hear His voice, harden not your hearts.*

What about our *today*? Is all well *today*? Is there anything in me *today* about which my Lord wants to speak to me? Let us not harden our hearts, but listen and obey.

September 20

Blessed be the God and Father of our Lord Jesus Christ,
who hath blessed us with all spiritual blessings
in heavenly places in Christ.
Eph. 1:3

And hath raised us up together, and made us sit together
in heavenly places in Christ Jesus.
Eph. 2:6

Some of us have watched with wonder a bird glide
in the high air. "If the wings are held outstretched without motion there will be an uplift if the air is full of little
motions, swirls and quiverings."

Let us practice using the "motions, swirls and quiverings" of life as means whereby we may attain to quietness of spirit.

God, who hast made sea gulls so beautiful,
    Cleaving the sky,
So let my service be— fearless and poised and sure —
    Teach me to fly.

God who hast taught sea gulls to soar and rest
    On empty space,
So let me rise to Thee, dwell in the heavenlies,
    Proving Thy grace.

September 21

*And hope maketh not ashamed; because the love of God is
shed abroad in our hearts by the Holy Ghost
which is given unto us.*
Rom. 5:5

This verse seems clearly to mean that love comes
first into our hearts. Then because love has come we
hope, and *that* hope "never disappoints," as Weymouth
puts it.

Experience worketh hope, Romans 5:4 tells us.
And so it does. But it also worketh fear. If we have had
long experience of the weakness of souls, and seen many
a time what seemed a great blaze-up of blessing fizzle
out, we do become fearful of hoping too much.

And yet the word stands. Here it is Way's para-
phrase (vv. 3–5): "I will go further, and say that we actually exult in such afflictions as ours, knowing as we
do that affliction develops unflinching endurance; that
endurance develops tested strength, and tested strength
develops the habit of hope. This hope is no delusive one,
as is proved by the fact that the brimming river of God's
love has already overflowed into our hearts, on-drawn
by His Holy Spirit, which He has given to us."

September 22

For if any be a hearer of the word, and not a doer, he is like unto a man beholding his natural face in a glass.
Jas. 1:23

Archbishop Benson said that James 1:23 meant: "If any man is a hearer of the word and not a doer, he is like unto a man who observeth the face of his birth in a mirror." He showed how "the study of God's word makes us see as in a mirror the face of our birth, the man that God meant us to be. If we remember that vision, and translate it at once into action, then we shall be gradually transformed according to God's loving purpose for us. But if, after seeing the vision, we go away and straightway forget what manner of man we were, then of course we shall not see the face of our birth quite so clearly next time" (*Speculum Animae*).

We all know that the Bible is the most wonderful book in the world. Various translations, such as Weymouth's, make it clear that more than just ordinary looking in the mirror is meant: "He is like a man who *carefully* looks at his own face in a mirror." More is meant than just a quick run through the appointed chapter or portion (if we use such helps to regularity). We must look closely and continue looking.

September 23

For I know whom I have believed, and am persuaded that
He is able to keep that which I have committed
unto Him against that day.
2 Tim. 1:12

We commit: He undertakes. And what He undertakes He carries through. We may have to wait to see
the fulfillment of our hope. We may be disappointed
again and again. But Love will find the way to fulfill the
promise of love.

2 Timothy 1:12 is a glorious word, and so is Hebrews 10:35: *Cast not away therefore your confidence,*
which hath great recompence of reward.

> O God of Hope, how green Thy trees,
> How calm each several star;
> Renew us, make us fresh like these,
> Calm as they are.
> O what can dim his hope who sees
> Though faintly and afar,
> The power that kindles green in trees
> And light in star?

❧

September 24

This also cometh forth from the Lord of hosts, which is
wonderful in counsel, and excellent in working.
Isa. 28:29

This also cometh forth from the Lord of hosts — whatever your "this" is, *this also* came forth from Him whom
you love. The word as first spoken is about our God's
care, in teaching us how to deal with the various kinds
of seed He gives us to use for food. Some are beaten,
some are ground. He teaches not only spiritual things,
but this also.

We may take the words for other things too. What
is my "this" today? What is my special need of help?
What is my weakness, my disappointment, my hope
deferred? What is my trial of faith? *This also cometh forth*
from the Lord.

❧

September 25

*To will is present with me; but how to perform
that which is good I find not.*
Rom. 7:18

*It is God which worketh in you both to will and
to do of His good pleasure.*
Phil. 2:13

I can do all things through Christ which strengtheneth me.
Phil. 4:13

Romans 7 is a description of our life as it was. It describes our life as it is whenever, even if only for one minute, we live the old self-life. But by His Spirit's enabling we are meant instead to live the Enoch life and walk with God.

The contrast between Romans 7:18 and Philippians 2:13 shows this glorious truth. I cannot, but God can. And so I can, and Philippians 4:13 becomes my experience.

There is just nothing we can do of ourselves, but *When I said, My foot slippeth; Thy mercy, O Lord, held me up* (Ps. 94:18).

So — I cannot . . . God can . . . I can.

September 26

*And when He cometh home, He calleth together His friends
and neighbors, saying unto them, Rejoice with Me;
for I have found My sheep which was lost.*
Luke 15:6

When a lost sheep is found, is it not wonderful to
be allowed to share in the home joy of the heavenly
people? It is as though our wonderful Savior said: "It is
not enough unless you all share it too — you, My dear
people on earth." So the joy of heaven overflows upon
us, like water from a brimming pool into which more
water is continually falling.

There is joy in the presence of the angels of God
over one sinner that repenteth (Luke 15:7) — and we
share that joy too.

September 27

And He said unto him, Well, thou good servant:
because thou hast been faithful in a very little,
have thou authority over ten cities.
Luke 19:17

We can do so little that the only words that describe what we do are just these words: *a very little.* But the Master was pleased with His servant because he had been faithful in a very little. He had been given one mina (the equivalent of three months wages) and now had ten minas.

The words are very searching too. Am I faithful as that servant was? He did not give five minas to his Master and keep five minas for himself, nor give nine minas to his Master and keep one mina for himself. Not even the smallest fraction of that ten minas was held back. All was given to his Master.

Am I faithful like that?

September 28

By love serve one another.
Gal. 5:13

Become bondservants to one another in a spirit of love.
(Weymouth):

The reward of faithfulness is always more responsible work, and this always means more difficult work. In the world it is different: the expected reward is more pay. The difficult work the trader of Luke 19:17 was given, as a reward for being faithful in a very little, was to become the servant of all the people of ten cities.

Sometimes we are working hard, and then we are given something still harder to do. We may be tempted then to wish for something easier, forgetting our Lord's way of rewards. How much easier to do business with money than to serve ten cities. The motto of the Prince of Wales, heir to the great authority of kingship, is *"I serve."*

The harder the work, the more we are thrown upon Him to whom all ten cities belong. *All souls are Mine,* the Lord said to Ezekiel (Ezek. 18:4). The more responsibility we bear for our Lord, the more necessary it is for us constantly to be with Him, to get to know His wishes. There is great comfort in this. Don't let us miss that comfort.

❧

September 29

In My Father's house are many mansions: if it were not so,
I would have told you. I go to prepare a place for you.
John 14:2

These words hold out a glorious hope. "Mansions" here does not mean big houses, but the resting places on the old Roman roads where a traveler was refreshed before setting forth again on his journey.

So we can picture the servants of the Lord who have been about His business here, serving Him later without any hindrance, and traveling for Him to far regions. (Where are all the people who have never heard of Him here? Perhaps we shall be sent to them.)

Westcott says that "the contrasted notions of repose and progress are combined in this vision of the future." We shall never be tired on those journeys, and we shall never fail.

And His servants shall serve Him: and they shall see His face; and His name shall be in their foreheads (Rev. 22:3–4). As we think of that, we shall not find it so hard to be *faithful in a very little* (Luke 19:17) for a short time here.

❧

September 30

And look that thou make them after their pattern,
which was shewed thee in the mount.
Exod. 25:40

What was the pattern for our work that was shown on the mount?

A work which was set on the glory of the Lord.

A work whose workers were all truly the Lord's.

A work full of love and joy and hope and peace.

A work hidden from the eye of man, but open to the eye of God, at all points searched by Him, lest at any time lesser aims should creep in.

A work whose needs are supplied by the Lord Himself, in answer to prayer based upon His own word.

This was the pattern which was shown on the mount. Lord, grant us grace to remember it and follow it.

Cause us to abound in hope, and to watch as those who must give account.

Hide us from the scourge of the tongue, but teach us how to find any help there is to be found in criticism and innuendo.

Make us far more intensely in earnest and cause us to press on — on to the goal.

October 1

*And he [Moses] said unto Him, If Thy presence go not
with me, carry us not up hence.*
Exod. 33:15

Are you dreading something that the month may
hold? There is no need to dread it *if you are carried
up to it*. Pray the prayer that Moses prayed, and you will
hear your Lord say to you what He said to Moses (Exod.
33:14), *My Presence shall go with thee, and I will give thee
rest*.

The disciples were full of fear when Jesus Himself
came *and stood in the midst, and saith unto them, Peace be
unto you* (John 20:19). He will stand in the midst of this
month, and of each day and each hour of the month,
and say to you, "Peace."

❧

October 2

And the men of the city said unto Elisha . . . the water is naught, and the ground barren. And he said, Bring me a new cruse, and put salt therein. And they brought it to him. And he went forth unto the spring of the waters, and cast the salt in there, and said, Thus saith the Lord, I have healed these waters; there shall not be from thence any more death or barren land.
2 Kings 2:19–21

All around the spring was ground which should have been fruitful, but the plants did not thrive. They grew for a while, but did not come to fruit. There was a general withering.

Suppose the spring had blamed the ground — "Such poor soil; no use watering it" — what would you have said? But have we never done just that? "Such difficult circumstances; it is not my fault if things go wrong. Such difficult people (or children), they aren't improving at all. I have spent ever so much time on them, and there is nothing to show for it."

The word about the spring was, *The water is naught.* It might flow over the ground forever, but nothing good would happen, for it was naught. Our influence may flow for years over people, but it will make no difference to them unless the spring within us is sweet. It must be healed from that quality which made it useless, and be turned into a source of life instead of death and barrenness.

October 3

The water is naught.
2 Kings 2:19

I am crucified with Christ: nevertheless I live; yet not I, but
Christ liveth in me: and the life which I now live in the flesh
I live by the faith of the Son of God, who loved me,
and gave Himself for me.
Gal. 2:20

Galatians 2:20 is the word of the spring that is healed. The water is naught, but when we truly trust the renewing force of the word of God, then His power makes that which is "naught" flow out in blessing to others.

The salt was put in a new cruse. The power comes to us by means of the word which is more than a mere word — some promise of our God which we have made our own.

What is your greatest need today? There is in this wonderful Book of ours the exact word that meets that need. Try it; prove it; stand on it. It will not fail you.

October 4

In all respects I try to prove the validity of my claim to be a steward of God's bounty — in many-sided endurance — amid afflictions, sore straits and privations, amid scourgings, prison-cells and riots, amid toils, night vigils, and fastings: in purity, in spiritual illumination, in long-suffering, in kindness, in the Holy Spirit's presence, in love unfeigned, in uttering the Message of Truth, in using the might of God.
2 Cor. 6:4–7 (Way)

Dr. Way's translation of the words "by the power of God" is *"in using* the might of God." If only we use the might of God, as the salt was used by Elisha (2 Kings 2:21), the water will be sweetened. It must be so.

Today the temptation will come to be impatient, or unpeaceful. The might of God is ready for our use. A look to Him brings it. We have His sure word (Isa. 26:3), *Thou wilt keep him in perfect peace, whose mind is stayed on Thee: because he trusteth in Thee.* To stand on that word is to use the might of God, for there is power in the word of God to effect what it says shall be.

Salt stings a wound, and if there is anything in us that is wrong, the word that He will bring to mind will sting before it heals. But if we are willing for that, the healing is sure. So let us use the might of God, and then all the influences that flow out from us will help others.

❧

October 5

And the work of righteousness shall be peace; and the effect of righteousness quietness and assurance for ever.
Isa. 32:17

This word will stand by us in any storm. If by the grace of God we do the right thing, whatever the trials of the time be, we shall be kept in peace. And that peace will abide, for *When He giveth quietness, who then can make trouble?* (Job 34:29).

"None have a right to joy but we, for joy is sown for us, and an ill summer will not spoil the crop," wrote Samuel Rutherford. The seed of joy is sown for us, and the seed of God is imperishable.

October 6

And they that are Christ's have crucified the flesh with the affections and lusts.
Gal. 5:24

But God forbid that I should glory, save in the cross of our Lord Jesus Christ, by whom the world is crucified unto me, and I unto the world.
Gal. 6:14

I am crucified with Christ.
Gal. 2:20

"I have preached much on a crucified life and the necessity of entering upon it, but were I to enter the pulpit again, I would preach upon it much more." Adolph Monod wrote that after some months of illness. One day in prayer he turned to his Lord: "I tremble sometimes at the prospect which lies before me. But no: Thou art Love. Thou art faithful. This crucified life, which I so often desired in the days of my health, Thou hast made it for me now, and I accept it in order that I may show that in the midst of this crucified life a Christian can find peace."

Illness such as his was is not the only form crucifixion can take. Sometimes it is in the smallest, most unseen things that Christ comes and says: "See in it a chance to die. Die to your own will, to your own thoughts and opinions, to your *I* in all its little private preferences."

For the greatest and deepest spiritual truth always meets us in the small practical matters of everyday common life.

October 7

Casting all your care upon Him; for He careth for you.
1 Pet. 5:7

Adolph Monod said that the poor often ask how the promise of God about their daily bread will be fulfilled. But when they look back over the years, they are astonished to see that He has provided for every day, often in ways they cannot remember.

It is the same with those who are ill: "When they look back over weeks, months, years, they are surprised to see that God has given them each day the promised strength." And Adolph Monod adds that "we ought to practice ourselves in casting away our anxieties."

That is a good word — *practice ourselves.* Practice will make us perfect in this. It will become natural to us to cast our care at once upon our Lord, instead of carrying it for a while ourselves, until tired out we turn to Him to find the rest that might have been ours at the beginning.

He cares for us. He who has loved *will* love; He who has led *will* lead; He who has kept *will* keep.

◈

October 8

Blessed be God, even the Father of our Lord Jesus Christ, the Father of mercies, and the God of all comfort.
2 Cor. 1:3

In one of his letters, Adolph Monod tells how he found in his hardest moments that it was enough to take firm hold on a single promise. It sustained him in the sorest difficulties. He loved the words *Father of Compassions,* as 2 Corinthians 1:3 has it in French.

When one is in great pain or trouble, or caught suddenly by fierce temptation, it is the word of strength or comfort that is set deep in the memory that takes life. It speaks in a new tone, and becomes to us at that moment more than we could have ever believed it would be. John 14:26 explains this: *But the Comforter, which is the Holy Ghost, . . . He shall teach you all things, and bring all things to your remembrance, whatsoever I have said unto you.*

So let us fill the storehouse of our mind with the treasure of God's word. Every day offers opportunities. When we go to bed tonight, let us think, "What treasure did I put in my storehouse today?"

October 9

My soul, wait thou only upon God;
for my expectation is from Him.
Ps. 62:5

"O may God preserve us," Pastor Monod wrote, "from making the word of man the first thing, and communion with Jesus a secondary matter."

We all know the temptation, when something distressing or perplexing happens, to turn to the nearest one, or the wisest and most loving, and talk the thing over with that one. It is right to do this. The help that often comes in this way is the good gift of the "Father of Compassions." But it does not take the place of the other. Communion with Jesus must come first. When it does not, we weaken and become discouraged. Perhaps we say something or write something better not said or written.

Our Lord is the great encourager of souls. Our expectation is from Him.

October 10

That thou mayest love the Lord thy God, and that thou mayest obey His voice, and that thou mayest cleave unto Him: for He is thy life, and the length of thy days.
Deut. 30:20

God of my Praise, to Thee be praise
For children and their loving ways;

For all the things that lighten earth,
For quiet peace, and merry mirth;

For every friendly bird that sings,
For little, lovely, simple things;

For loyal comradeship that grows
The stronger for each wind that blows;

But most of all because Thou art
The sunshine of my happy heart.

God of my Praise, to Thee be praise,
Today and through my length of days.

October 11

*Know thou the God of thy father, and serve Him with
a perfect heart and with a willing mind: for the Lord
searcheth all hearts, and understandeth all the imaginations
of the thoughts: if thou seek Him, He will be found of thee.*
1 Chron. 28:9

Serve Him with a willing mind. That means, Do not
long for what is not given. Trust Me. Look on. Press on.
Serve Me with a willing mind.

The word is a call to faith and to obedience. We
are called to serve with a willing mind just where we
are, and just as things are. We may not be able to see
the meaning of anything, or to catch the least glimpse
of the gladness on before. Don't let us disappoint our
God. He trusts us to trust. He loves the offering of a
willing mind.

The Lord searches our hearts, and knows all our
imaginations, all our thoughts. If we seek Him, He will
reveal Himself to us in all His love and beauty.

❧

October 12

God is able to make all grace abound toward you; that ye,
always having all sufficiency in all things,
may abound to every good work.
2 Cor. 9:8

"All, always, all, all." Truly "God is able to lavish every gracious gift upon you," as Way puts it.

Sometimes one special verse is brought twice or perhaps oftener to our notice. It is because it has a word for us that we might miss if we were not redirected to it. This is part of the kindness of God to whom nothing that concerns us is small.

When David asks in Psalm 60:9: *Who will bring me into the strong city? who will lead me into Edom?* the fortified city was probably Petra, the capital of Edom. There was only one way into Petra, and it was a long and difficult way. But where it began, and where it ended, there were pink oleanders.

The strong words of 2 Corinthians 9:8 are like the oleanders at the entrance to the difficult way that leads into the city of Petra. They are full of good cheer and promise of good things to come. When the traveler penetrates that forbidding gorge and comes out into the sunshine, he finds oleanders blooming again for him. When we by His grace pass through whatever trial or difficulty faces us now, we shall find this word waiting to refresh us again. *All, always, all, all — that we may abound to every good work.*

October 13

*Therefore seeing we have this ministry, as we have received
mercy, we faint not; but have renounced
the hidden things of dishonesty.
2 Cor. 4:1–2*

"They build the front just like St. Mark's,
  Or like Westminster Abbey;
And then, as if to cheat the Lord,
  They make the back parts shabby."

Are the backs of our houses as tidy as the fronts? Are
the parts of our character and of our ways which no one
can see as right as those which all can see? Are we true
right through? The people who built in that deceitful
way, making the back parts shabby, had not renounced
the hidden things of dishonesty.

"I have renounced all underhand dealings" is Way's
version; and Weymouth gives a further thought: "We
have renounced the secrecy which marks a feeling of
shame."

Isn't it a comfort that we have a Bible prayer that
says just what we want to say to God: Psalm 139:23–24.
*Search me, O God, and know my heart: try me, and know
my thoughts: and see if there be any wicked way in me, and
lead me in the way everlasting.*

❧

October 14

*Jesus saith to Simon Peter, Simon, son of Jonas, lovest thou
Me more than these? He saith unto Him, Yea, Lord;
Thou knowest that I love Thee.
He saith unto him, Feed My lambs.*
John 21:15

Three hundred years ago Samuel Rutherford wrote:
"No greater testimony of our love to Christ can be, than
to feed carefully and faithfully His lambs." And Père
Didon wrote: "We have a great need nowadays of self-
sacrificing souls to teach the young generation by their
very lives."

The little children of Jerusalem, exactly like little
children everywhere, noticed what their elders did, and
did it too. They did in the afternoon what their elders
had done on Palm Sunday morning — *The children
were crying in the temple, and saying, Hosanna to the Son
of David* (Matt. 21:15). Children generally reflect those
who are about them. Their clear eyes look through what
we say to what we are.

Often there is nothing of sacrifice in our task of
bringing up children. But our Lord Jesus knew what it
would cost Peter to feed His lambs, and He knows what
it costs some of us. He overlooks nothing, forgets nothing. And He says of each hidden sacrificial act, *Ye have
done it unto Me* (Matt. 25:40).

October 15

And Peter calling to remembrance saith unto Him, Master,
behold, the fig tree which Thou cursedst is withered away.
Mark 11:21

"Half the misery in the world comes from trying to
look, instead of trying to be, what one is not." George
Macdonald said that. The fig tree did that on Monday
(Mark 11:12–14). On Tuesday it was dried up from the
roots.

The disciples had a chance then to learn, not only
what faith in God meant, but also what a tremendous
thing in His sight insincerity is. The fruitless tree in full
leaf was a picture of that, for when a fig tree is in full leaf
we may expect fruit.

The story is full of meaning for us who have to help
others. We cannot give them what we have not got ourselves. We may seem to be able to give, but they will
soon discover whether or not there are figs under our
leaves. If there are none, the awful penalty is to dry up
from the roots — that is, to be unable to give anything
to anyone.

God save us from that! It need never be our fate.
The blessed opposite of the fig-tree story is the parable
of the Vine in John 15:1–5.

October 16

Verily, verily, I say unto thee, When thou wast young, thou girdedst thyself, and walkedst whither thou wouldest: but when thou shalt be old, thou shalt stretch forth thy hands, and another shall gird thee, and carry thee whither thou wouldest not. This spake He, signifying by what death he should glorify God.
John 21:18–19

When thou wast young . . . but when thou shalt be old. Babes in Christ are nursed, not crucified. They have certain liberties — *Thou walkest whither thou wouldest.* But when they grow up into spiritual manhood all that is changed.

And yet, they would not go back to the other easier life, for they are nearer their Lord now, far nearer than ever they were before.

October 17

Mortify therefore your members which are upon the earth.
Col. 3:5

Most of us know what it is to "crucify" some desire, or other form of self, and then to find it come to life again. A medical illustration makes the meaning of Colossians 3:5 clear. Something that is not wanted is touched by something that withers it up, like caustic, or an acid. If it reappears it is touched again.

Weymouth's version is, "Put to death your earthward inclinations." As the desire for anything not given to you appears, look to the Good Physician to touch it with death. (The drop of acid is death to the thing it touches.) If it appears again, ask Him to touch it again. He will never say, "You asked Me before." He will not tire till that desire is withered to the root.

October 18

Neither murmur ye, as some of them also murmured,
and were destroyed of the destroyer.
1 Cor. 10:10

"Neither let us murmur at restrictions" is Way's translation. A murmuring spirit is like a fretting leprosy. It can only end in destruction.

The foolishness of man perverteth (overthroweth) *his way: and his heart fretteth against the Lord* (Prov. 19:3). When we let ourselves fret against the restrictions that hamper us, we are fretting against the Lord. He could as easily remove them as we could open a door.

Let us pray today for a merry heart, whatever our restrictions, for *A merry heart doeth good like a medicine* (Prov. 17:22).

October 19

The Lord thy God in the midst of thee is mighty; He will save, He will rejoice over thee with joy; He will be silent in His love, He will joy over thee with singing.
Zeph. 3:17 (margin)

Sometimes after a period of special prayer there is a silence. We are not conscious of any response on the part of God.

We can give Him joy by not misunderstanding His silence. He loves us to count on His tender caring, His deep solicitude, even though, for reasons that we may not know, He is for a while silent in His love.

We grieve our Father when we allow discouraged thoughts to prevail. "Does He care so very much? He has not said anything to me. He has not answered." Love is a very tender thing. A thought can hurt it. But just because it is so tender, a very little thing can give it infinite joy. Our little, constant communications of love give real joy to our Father's heart.

❧

October 20

*The Spirit of the Lord is upon Me, because He hath anointed
Me to preach the gospel to the poor; He hath sent Me to heal
the brokenhearted, to preach deliverance to the captives,
and recovering of sight to the blind,
to set at liberty them that are bruised.*
Luke 4:18

Sometimes, when we fail and have to ask for forgiveness, we are terribly tempted to weakness. We have failed so often that we wonder whether we can ever be more than conquerors.

But to be forgiven is to be strengthened, for "He hath anointed Me... *to strengthen with forgiveness* those that are bruised." The words are from the Aramaic Gospel, the very oldest (so some believe) of all the written Gospels. So the words may indeed be the very words our Lord Jesus spoke, for He spoke in Aramaic. Are they not beautiful and comforting?

❧

October 21

And whosoever shall compel thee to go a mile,
go with him twain.
Matt. 5:41

We all know how we love people who are continually running the second mile. They are very nice to live with. They heap all sorts of loving little extras on top of the day's work. They seem to be always on the lookout for people who want them to run that tiring second mile, and then off they go, as if to be allowed to run it was the happiest thing in the world.

Have you ever looked at them and thought, "I would like to be like that, but . . ." And then you remembered some trouble of your own, and it felt such a burden that you began to think it would be as much as you could do to get through your first mile without attempting a second.

The Aramaic of Matthew 5:41 says: "Whosoever compels you to carry a burden for a mile, go with him twain." Our Lord is always asking the impossible of us. He is always trusting us to rise to it. And best of all, He is always standing alongside to make the impossible possible. *I can do all things through Christ which strengtheneth me* (Phil. 4:13).

October 22

And when He had sent them away,
He departed into a mountain to pray.
Mark 6:46

"He then bade the people farewell, and went away up the hill to pray" (Weymouth). "Having said 'goodbye' to them all, He went away into the mountain to pray."

Today there will be a strong pull to hold us back from this detachment. The great adversary knows that everything depends on our frequently saying "goodbye" to things and people, in order to escape to the place where our God can pour His life into us. We need to spend time alone with Him, so that He can make us strong to live undefeated by temptation, and triumphant over circumstances.

The Lord enable us to make this "goodbye" to the habit of our lives, today and every day.

&

October 23

Blessed are they that mourn: for they shall be comforted.
Matt. 5:4

What comfort is there, if you have lost a beloved child, a husband or wife, a father or mother, or other close relative or friend?

Will this help? If our Lord Jesus came into our garden and asked for a flower, would we choose a faded flower, or one we did not like and did not want, to give to Him? We know we could never do that.

He has come to our garden. He has asked for one of our sweetest flowers. Do we grudge Him that flower? Do we wish He had chosen another? In our hearts we know that if we really saw Him come we would say, "Lord Jesus, take our best."

Then let us say that to Him now. He will take good care of our flower.

October 24

Pray for them which despitefully use you.
Luke 6:28

Are there any who are making your burdens heavier than they need be? Sometimes very small things can make our burdens feel heavier. The temptation always is to resent this, and feel ruffled.

The Lord Jesus says to us, "Pray for those who compel you to carry burdens." Don't talk about them to others, unless that talk will bear the scrutiny of the Lord Jesus Christ. Don't talk about them to yourself. Look up to your Father for them. Pray that *their* burdens may be lightened. (Perhaps they have some of which you know nothing.) Pray, and as you pray, love will flow into your heart for them.

October 25

But I will deliver thee in that day, saith the Lord: and thou
shalt not be given into the hand of the men
of whom thou art afraid.
Jer. 39:17

What is the thing you most fear and most earnestly pray about, the thing that you most dread? If you love your Lord and yet know your own weakness, it is that something may happen to sweep you off your feet, or that your strength may be drained and you may yield and fall, and fail Him at the end. The lives of many are shadowed by this fear.

But take comfort. The God who knew the heart of His servant Ebed-melech knows our heart too. He knows who the men are (what the forces of trial are) of whom we are afraid. And He assures us and reassures us. The Bible is full of "Fear nots." *Thou shalt not be given into the hand of the men of whom thou art afraid.*

ᆺ

October 26

*And I will strengthen the house of Judah, and I will save the
house of Joseph, and I will bring them again to place them;
for I have mercy upon them: and they shall be as though I
had not cast them off: for I am the Lord their God, and will
hear them. And they of Ephraim shall be like a mighty man,
and their heart shall rejoice as through wine:
yea, their children shall see it, and be glad;
their heart shall rejoice in the Lord.
Zech. 10:6–7*

There are wonderful words of assurance and comfort scattered about in the prophets, which seem to be
written specially for discouraged hours. Even though
they refer first to the return of the Jews to their own
land, they are for us too, in a spiritual sense. They lift us
up when we are cast down and feel "cast off." They are
among God's glorious "Fear nots."

Have you noticed the perfect ending to today's
promise? God knows that it is our children's good that
we most desire. And so He says, *Their children shall see
it, and be glad.*

October 27

Thou therefore endure hardness, as a good soldier of Jesus
Christ. No man that warreth entangleth himself with the
affairs of this life; that he may please him
who hath chosen him to be a soldier.
2 Tim. 2:3–4

Père Didon, who died at Toulouse in 1900, wrote letters to prepare and strengthen a woman for work among little girls. A few years later, after great public service, and much suffering, he gave himself to the education of young boys. This is what he wrote about those who wanted to work for the Lord among children:

"I do not want people who come to me under certain reservations. In battle you need soldiers who fear nothing. Enlarge yourself then, and may noble sacrifices never appear to you too burdensome. Tear yourself away from self — that is the work of the strong. The really great hearts are those who have learned to forget self. So long as one is occupied with self, one is petty and unworthy of Christ who humbled Himself even unto death to prove how much He loved us.

"Never say to yourself, 'It is enough,' but keep rising higher. Feelings are of very little value; the will is everything. God will not take you to task for your feelings, for it is not within the power of man to ward them off, or allay them. That which God looks at in the human soul is the will. The only thing that lies within our power is to will, to love. That is what Christ wants of us; that is the important thing. He reckons us only according to the measure of our will and our love."

❧

October 28

Hope in the Lord, and do good; and dwell on the land,
and thou shalt be fed with the wealth of it.
Ps. 37:3 (Septuagint)

There is endless wealth for us, and many kinds of wealth. The beauty of the world is one; the love which makes life such a joy is another; but the Hebrew of Psalm 37:3 gives us the richest treasure of all. *Feed on faithfulness* (see RV margin). That is, says Kay, the faithfulness of God.

There are various ways of feeding on faithfulness. One way is found in Bible reading. How do we read? In snippets? In little bits chosen for the lambs of the flock? That is good while we are lambs, but it is not enough for us after we grow up into Christ.

"I read a chapter a day," say some, and feel that is quite enough. It is not enough.

Are you in earnest to be fed? *The soul of the sluggard desireth, and hath nothing: but the soul of the diligent shall be made fat* (Prov. 13:4). Our Father wants His children to be diligent, to take trouble to find what He has stored up for them. He loves to give, but the sluggish soul cannot receive. It is too sleepy, too lazy, too contented with itself to be strengthened and enriched and made a blessing to others.

May God give us a new diligence, so that as we read we shall be fed and strengthened and made strong to help others.

October 29

*The slothful man roasteth not that which he took in hunting:
but the substance of a diligent man is precious.*
Prov. 12:27

The slothful man roasteth not that which he took in hunting describes the kind of Bible reading that fills notebooks with notes, but stops at that. Everything is meant to be turned to some use. What we learn is meant to be given to others, sooner or later. Commands are meant to be obeyed; promises are meant to be trusted and lived upon.

What are we doing with what we find in our Bibles? What about that beautiful verse found and marked yesterday? Did we turn it into life? Did we use it as a precious substance for our nourishment in weakness, or encouragement in difficulty, or victory in temptation, or joy in weariness, or peace in strife? *The substance of a diligent man is precious,* it counts for something. It must not be left like the talent in the napkin to do nothing for anyone.

October 30

But He giveth more grace.
Jas. 4:6

Have you ever felt as if you were coming to the Lord too often, asking for too much? There are many words that meet that feeling. Here is one: *He giveth more.* He is never tired of giving more, so we need never fear to ask. He is ready; He delights to give; He gives more.

The noun in the text is "grace": *He giveth more grace.* But grace is a word which encompasses everything. What do you want today? Patience? *He giveth more.* Love? *He giveth more.* Strength? *He giveth more.*

❧

October 31

And this is the confidence that we have in Him, that, if we ask
anything according to His will, He heareth us: and if we know
that He hear us, whatsoever we ask, we know that
we have the petitions that we desired of Him.
1 John 5:14–15

When we pray Bible prayers we know that we are asking according to God's will, and so we have great confidence. We know that He hears, and we know that we *have* what we desired of Him.

Here is a prayer to pray clause by clause, Colossians 1:9–11 as translated by Dr. Way:

"I ask God that you may have in full measure that perfect knowledge of His will which is an essential of all true wisdom, of all spiritual intelligence.

"I ask Him that you may pass through life in a manner worthy of our Lord, so as to please Him entirely.

"I ask that in every good work you may, as trees of His planting, still be bearing fruit, still growing higher, in the perfect knowledge of God.

"I ask Him that with all His strength you may be strengthened, even to the measure of the might of His divine majesty, till you attain to all-enduring patience and forbearance, which exults under suffering.

"I ask that you may ever render thanksgiving to the Father, who has made us fit to have a share in the inheritance of His consecrated ones who walk in light."

November 1

There is no fear in love; but perfect love casteth out fear:
because fear hath torment. He that feareth
is not made perfect in love.
1 John 4:18

Let us take time today to consider the love of God. Some of us are tempted to fear about ourselves. What about tomorrow? Shall we be able to go on? *Perfect love casteth out fear.* Love God and there will be no room for fear, for to love is to trust and if we trust we do not fear.

Some of us are tempted to fear the future. There again perfect love casts out fear. He who has led will lead. It quickens love and encourages faith to think of all that God has done. He has not brought us so far, to leave us now.

So let us open all our windows and our doors to the great love of God. Love is like light. It will flood our rooms if only we open to it. Let us take time today to open more fully than ever before to the blessed love of God.

❧

November 2

O let not mine heart be inclined to any evil thing: let me not
be occupied in ungodly works with
the men that work wickedness.
Ps. 141:4 (BCP)

This verse speaks of *inclination* and *occupation*. Miles Coverdale lived from 1488 to 1569, and the history of that period, when he was translating the Scriptures and giving us the version of the Psalms which we have in the Episcopal Prayer Book, is one of falseness and cruelty and utter disregard of all true goodness. The nations of the world were inclined to and occupied in works that had nothing to do with the holiness of God.

But even then God had His own, and as they prayed this prayer He heard them and He answered them. They were the salt of the earth. They were the candles set in the house of that dark age.

Is it not good to think that we may belong to that company? On what are my inclinations set? On pleasing my Lord? If so, He will see to it that my occupations are His pleasure only.

O let not our hearts be inclined to any evil thing today, for as our inclinations, so will be our occupations.

November 3

Hear, O earth: behold, I will bring evil upon this people,
even the fruit of their thoughts, because they have not hear-
kened unto My words, nor to My law, but rejected it.
Jer. 6:19

Each seed brings forth its own fruit, and each
thought brings forth its own fruit too. In the sorrowful
verse from which this phrase comes — *the fruit of their*
thoughts — God says that because people would not listen to His words, but rejected them, evil would come
upon them. That evil was not something brought upon
them from outside. It was the fruit of their thoughts.
Seed is hidden in the ground, and yet brings forth something that we can see. Just so the thought hidden in our
minds brings forth something which can be seen. It will
be good or bad according to the nature of the seed.

What are my thoughts? What do I think about
most, especially when I am alone? What sort of seed am
I sowing? What sort of fruit shall I gather from the seed
I am sowing today?

November 4

Try me, O God, and seek the ground of my heart:
prove me, and examine my thoughts.
Ps. 139:23 (BCP)

My meditation of Him shall be sweet:
I will be glad in the Lord.
Ps. 104:34

If we ask God to search the ground of our hearts, where we sow the seed of our thoughts, He will answer that prayer. He will purify the ground and give us good seed to sow there. So we shall come to that wonderful prayer, "Let my meditation be sweet to Him" (Septuagint).

We could never have dreamed of such a prayer ourselves. *Our* thoughts, sweet to our Lord! It can only be because He has first given the thoughts. We could not find them for ourselves, any more than we could make the seeds that we sow in our gardens.

There is another joy folded up in those words. Such seed must have sweet fruit, and this fruit is ours to give to others.

So let us be careful about our thinking. "It doesn't matter what I think" is a fatal word. It does matter.

❧

November 5

And now, little children, abide in Him; that, when He shall appear, we may have confidence, and not be ashamed before Him at His coming.
1 John 2:28

Could there be anything more joyful than to see Him and not be ashamed? Some of us find it difficult to believe that this can ever be. It could never be if it were not that when He forgives, He forgives wholly.

It is written that the sea shall give up the dead which are in it (Rev. 20:13), but it is never written that the sea shall give up the sins that were cast into its depths. Let the troubled heart rest on Micah 7:19 and Isaiah 44:22 and 1 John 1:9 and many another scripture, and then there will be courage to believe that even we, by His grace, shall have confidence and not be ashamed before Him at His coming.

❧

November 6

My soul followeth hard after Thee:
Thy right hand upholdeth me.
Ps. 63:8

My soul hangeth upon Thee.
(BCP)

Hindu India is divided into two great schools of thought. One school finds an illustration of what it believes in the baby monkey clinging to his mother. The other finds its illustration in the mother cat holding her kitten. Psalm 63:8 unites the two thoughts, for both are true, and both together make the whole truth.

My soul hangeth upon Thee — the monkey hold. *Thy right hand upholdeth me* — the cat hold.

Am I tempted to be slack about my Quiet Times, or about something which nobody sees, but which weakens me? Then the word for me is Hold on; don't be slack. Be in earnest. *My soul hangeth upon Thee. My soul followeth hard after Thee.*

Am I tired, tempted to fear, tempted to discouragement? There is no need to fear. "Underneath are the everlasting arms" (Deut. 33:27). *Thy right hand upholdeth me.*

November 7

The river of God is full of water.
Ps. 65:9 (RV)

Recently I was sent a picture of a jug into which water was being poured. The idea was that love, or whatever we need, is poured into us like that. I don't think of it so at all. I think of the love of God as a great river, pouring through us as the waters pour through our ravine in flood time. Nothing can keep this love from pouring through us, except of course our own blocking of the river.

Do you sometimes feel that you have got to the end of your love for someone who refuses and repulses you? Such a thought is folly, for one cannot come to the end of what one has not got. We have no store of love at all. We are not jugs, we are riverbeds.

If there be hindrance, sweep it all away;
O Love Eternal, pour through me I pray.

November 8

Hear me when I call, O God of my righteousness:
Thou hast enlarged me when I was in distress.
Ps. 4:1

Stand in awe, and sin not: commune with your own heart
upon your bed, and be still.
Ps. 4:4

Offer the sacrifices of righteousness,
and put your trust in the Lord.
Ps. 4:5

Thou hast put gladness in my heart, more than in the time
that their corn and their wine increased.
Ps. 4:7

Rotherham's rendering of verse 1 is, "When I cry, answer me O mine own righteous God." Let that *mine own* sink in. I am nothing, but I am His own. He understands His own. "In a strait place Thou hast made room for me." David remembers the years of the right hand of the Most High. There is nothing that more quickly reinforces faith than to remember the love of my Lord in the past. He is as He was yesterday.

Sometimes our prayer is interrupted, and we have to stop and turn to those who are making trouble. It is so here, in verses 2 and 3, but verse 4 has a wise word for us, "Be deeply moved but do not sin" (Rotherham). We must be deeply moved often. *Who is offended, and I burn not?* said Paul (2 Cor. 11:29).

But beware of anything personal slipping in. So be quiet again, says the Psalm. There is wonderful gain to be found in stillness. Then in verse 5: Do whatever you ought to do. It may be extremely difficult, but do it, and put your trust in the Lord who has said, *The work of righteousness shall be peace; and the effect of righteousness quietness and assurance for ever* (Isa. 32:17).

If there is talk again (verse 6), take it to your God and seek the light of His countenance. If you have that, what matter a million frowns? Only gladness and peace can follow.

❧

November 9

*Thou dost wonderfully shine forth from
the everlasting mountains.*
Ps. 76:4 (Septuagint)

*For the inward thought of man shall give thanks to Thee;
and the memorial of his inward thought
shall keep a feast to Thee.*
Ps. 76:10 (Septuagint)

There is nothing in all creation, and so nothing even in you and me, that can discourage the Lord the Conqueror. Because He does wonderfully shine forth, therefore our inward thoughts can give thanks and keep a feast to Him.

There are caterpillars with skins so transparent that we can see the green of the leaves they have been feeding on, their "inward thoughts." Suppose our minds had transparent skins so that our thoughts could be seen, what would be seen? Self-loving thoughts? Self-pitying thoughts? Lazy thoughts about our work? Unkind thoughts about others? Would these be seen?

Or would our happy thoughts be seen keeping a feast to God? Think of it — all our big thoughts and little thoughts, like big children and little at a birthday party, keeping a feast, singing and praising and being glad because of our loving God!

❧

November 10

*And Abraham said of Sarah his wife, She is my sister:
and Abimelech, king of Gerar sent and took Sarah. And
Abimelech said unto Abraham, What sawest thou, that thou
hast done this thing? And Abraham said, Because I thought,
Surely the fear of God is not in this place.*
Gen. 20:2, 10–11

*And God said unto him [Abimelech] in a dream, Yea, I
know that thou didst this in the integrity of thy heart.*
Gen. 20:6

Twice over we read that Abraham misjudged men.
Because of that hard judgment he fell into sin himself,
and grievously dishonored his God. In Genesis 20:11
we have Abraham's *I thought,* and in verse 6 God's *I
know.* God's knowledge is far kinder than Abraham's
thought.

This is a plea for the gentle judgment of children
and immature souls. A very special baptism of love is
needed if mistakes of judgment are to be avoided, for
love gives understanding. Nothing else does.

Lord, give us this love today.

November 11

Ye are of God, little children, and have overcome them:
because greater is He that is in you than
he that is in the world.
1 John 4:4

Nothing is impossible for the devil to attempt: nothing is impossible for the Lord to achieve; for greater is He that is in you than he that is in the world.

Notice the difference in the verbs, *attempt, achieve.*

November 12

*Behold, Thou wast wroth, and we sinned: in them have
we been of long time, and shall we be saved? For we are all
become as one that is unclean, and all our righteousnesses are
as a polluted garment: and we all do fade as a leaf; and our
iniquities, like the wind, take us away. And there is none
that calleth upon Thy name, that stirreth up himself to take
hold of Thee.... But now, O Lord, Thou art our father;
we are the clay, and Thou our potter;
and we all are the work of Thy hand.*
Isa. 64:5–8 (RV)

Isaiah speaks of a great need of salvation. The Re-
vised Version makes the meaning clear. In our sins *have
we been of long time.* Honest words about our condition
follow, and then the blessed, healing *But now,* regarding
the eternal mercy of God. *But now, O Lord, Thou art
our Father.*

Are you discouraged because of something wrong
that has been "of long time"? Thank God there is no
need to be discouraged. You may have to "stir yourself
up to take hold." It will mean an effort of will and an
act of faith. But *It is God which worketh in you both to
will and to do of His good pleasure* (Phil. 2:13). And He
is our Father.

*But when he was yet a great way off, his father saw
him, and had compassion, and ran, and fell on his neck,
and kissed him* (Luke 15:20).

November 13

My heart standeth in awe of Thy word. I rejoice at Thy word, as one that findeth great spoil.
Ps. 119:161–162

Did you ever notice this curious thing about Bible reading? Wherever you read, if only you go on reading and don't stop at the end of the chapter because it is the end, you come upon the very word you most need at that moment.

And did you ever notice this? It doesn't matter whether you read according to Scripture Union Notes or some other system, or some way of your own, your reading seems to have been arranged specially for you, so that one portion fits with another.

We do truly find great spoil in God's word, which makes us rejoice. But let us remember what comes first: *My heart standeth in awe of Thy word.* And *If ye love Me, keep My commandments* (John 14:15). If we love we do as the loved one wishes: "A wish is a command to one who loves."

November 14

Surely in vain the net is spread in the sight of any bird
Prov. 1:17

When God is speaking to a soul, the devil always tries to spread a net to entangle him. Have you ever heard a message and found yourself thinking, "Yes, that is just the word for him. It fits him exactly. I hope he will take it to heart." If you have, then you know one of Satan's favorite nets. He tries to make us think of somebody else, and pass the message on to him, instead of taking it for ourselves.

But surely in vain the net is spread in the sight of any bird. If you see the net, pray this prayer: "Lord, open my ears to hear what Thou wilt say to me. Make me sincere, and give me grace to obey."

And then, *Whatsoever He saith unto you, do it* (John 2:5).

November 15

The Lord is a God of knowledge,
and by Him actions are weighed.
1 Sam. 2:3

"It was a wonderful meeting. I felt greatly helped."
Have you been caught in the net of that sort of talk? To
be full of feelings but not to do anything about what has
been heard is to be entangled in the devil's net.

1 Samuel 2:3 shows that with God not feelings but
actions are weighed. What have you done? What are
you going to do? Are you in earnest to do whatever your
Lord says to you? Then set your will to do it. Look up to
the Strong for strength, and take His all-sufficient grace
to help you to obey today.

❧

November 16

*They shall be abundantly satisfied with the fatness of
Thy house; and Thou shalt make them drink
of the river of Thy pleasures.*
Ps. 36:8

The Septuagint has "They shall be fully satisfied,"
and a footnote says that the Greek means "intoxicated."
It is not difficult to be "abundantly satisfied" or even
"intoxicated" with God's goodness when all is going
well. But when things are, as we say, "impossibly hard,"
what then?

Well, the word still stands, and we must learn to
live in the power of that word: *They shall be abundantly
satisfied with the fatness of Thy house.* In other words,
satisfied with Him, His will, His providence, His provi-
sion, His withholdings as well as His givings. We must
not build our satisfaction, our happiness, on any earthly
thing; not on having what we want, or going where we
want, or doing what we want.

The foundation of our happiness must be invisible,
not visible. It must not depend on circumstances of any
sort whatever. Let us gratefully take all that is given us
of visible good things, for they are the gift of our most
loving Father. But do not let us build on these things.
No, never.

❧

November 17

Jesus saith unto them, Believe ye that I am able to do this?
They said unto Him, Yea, Lord.
Matt. 9:28

Jesus said unto her, . . . Whosoever liveth and believeth in Me
shall never die. Believest thou this? She saith unto Him, Yea,
Lord: I believe that Thou art the Christ, the Son of God.
John 11:25–27

Simon, Son of Jonas, lovest thou Me? He saith unto Him,
Yea, Lord; Thou knowest that I love Thee.
John 21:16

I used to have a slip of wood on my wall with these words painted on it: YES, LORD. *Believe ye that I am able to do this?* meant the hardest thing I had to trust for at that time. The *Yes, Lord,* on the wall was a great help.

Later I came to the *Yes, Lord,* of Martha, which led to so much, and to Peter's *Yes, Lord, Thou knowest that I love Thee.* At every point in my life, one or another of these three *Yes, Lord*s has been a word of life and peace.

"Do you believe that I am able to do this?"
Yes, Lord.
"Do you believe this word that I have spoken to you?"
Yes, Lord.
"Do you love Me?"
Yes, Lord.

November 18

God anointed Jesus of Nazareth with the Holy Ghost and with power: who went about doing good, and healing all that were oppressed of the devil; for God was with Him.
Acts 10:38

"I saw a human life ablaze with God,
    I felt a power divine,
As through an empty vessel of frail clay
    I saw God's glory shine.
Then woke I from a dream and cried aloud,
    'My Father, give to me
The blessing of a life consumed by God
    That I may live for Thee.'"

These words hold the prayer of our hearts. Sometimes we are tempted to think that the ordinary things of life do not give much opportunity for God to answer such a prayer. But they do. As we read through the Gospels, we cannot help noticing the ordinariness of much of our Lord's life on earth. Nobody described Him as going about ablaze with God. He *went about doing good,* and yet was ever a life so "consumed by God"?

Let no one be discouraged. "He never passes us without a word and a smile," was said about someone the other day. That word and that smile has helped many a soul through its battles. Such lives burn and shine.

November 19

We are troubled on every side, yet not distressed;
we are perplexed, but not in despair.
2 Cor. 4:8

Is anything trying to shatter your faith and peace today? If so, test and prove those two words, *Yet... But.* They will not give way under your feet. Add to them the *But God* of Psalm 73:26, and you will never fail.

My flesh and my heart faileth: but God is the strength of my heart, and my portion for ever.

&

November 20

Then Jesus answered and said, ... Bring him hither to Me.
Matt. 17:17

Have you a "him" about whom you are anxious?
Bring him to Me. Have you a "her"? Bring her to Me.
We can even turn the pronoun to "it" — this crushing
burden of the state of the world, the grief and misery
that overwhelms us if we think at all — Bring it to Me.
We can turn the word to "all" — the problems of our
work with its cares and its questions, and more personal
cares and anxieties too — Bring all to Me.

And there are joys, too. Don't let us bring only
griefs and anxieties, but also thanks and praises.

Bring *him* to Me.

Bring *her* to Me.

Bring *it* to Me.

Bring *all* to Me.

❧

November 21

A good man out of the good treasure of the heart bringeth forth good things: and an evil man out of the evil treasure bringeth forth evil things.
Matt. 12:35

That Thou givest them they gather: Thou openest Thine hand, they are filled with good (Ps. 104:28). Look at God's birds. They are busy all day long, gathering what they have been given, and they chirp and sing as they gather. I have a little sunbird, whose wings a cruel man cut so that it can't fly. He chirps every time he sips sugar and water, and he flicks his little tail. It is his way of saying, Thank you.

Do you flick your tail? Don't laugh and say, "I haven't got a tail." Your tail is in your mouth. It is your tongue. Use it.

Our heavenly Father gives us good treasures out of His heavenly store. What do we say about it? He likes us to say "Thank you" to the one through whose hand it comes, and to be grateful to Him, our dear Father.

Grateful; thankful; these are nice words. We can't possibly say "Thank you" all the time. We wouldn't have time for anything else if we did. But we can be full of thanks always — thankful, grateful.

Am I? Are you?

November 22

Remember the words of the Lord Jesus, how He said,
It is more blessed to give than to receive.
Acts 20:35

We are in this world to give, not to receive. It is true that we receive countless good things every day. (Have you ever tried to count them?) As we grow older, we shall want to do as our Lord did, strip ourselves of all we can, so that we may have more to give to others. He was rich, yet for our sakes He became poor (2 Cor. 8:9). He has left us an example.

A small child nearly always wants to get and keep as much as it can. I remember a tiny child seizing three balls, and as she could not hold three in her hands she sat on one, to make sure of it. But that desire to "have" passes, if we follow our Lord.

There are many things we would like to have, and to do. But we turn away from them for Christ's sake and for the sake of others, not grudgingly but very joyfully.

May we be His very happy givers today.

❧

November 23

*For we are His workmanship, created in Christ Jesus unto
good works, which God hath before ordained
that we should walk in them.*
Eph. 2:10

This is a tremendous thought. We were created to do certain things which God thought about and planned long before we knew anything about them. There is eternal blessing in doing these things. There is no blessing at all in doing any other things. It would be dreadful if we overlooked the things our Father meant us to do, and instead did something we chose ourselves.

There is one place in all the world that has been already prepared for you today. In no other place is there blessing. In no other work is there blessing.

If you are already fitted into that place, and doing the work planned for you, then carry on with joy and without fear.

November 24

Lord, who shall abide in Thy tabernacle? who shall dwell in
Thy holy hill? He that backbiteth not with his tongue,
nor doeth evil to his neighbor,
nor taketh up a reproach against his neighbor.
Ps. 15:1, 3

Sir Robert Ball, the astronomer, began when he was old to write the story of his life. He made this rule for himself: "Try to give everything narrated a kind twist."

Isn't that a beautiful rule? Let us ask the Spirit of God to search us about this matter of giving a "kind twist" to what others say and do.

Do you know this rhyme? What does it mean to us?
"A twister of twists once twisted a twist,

And the twist that he twisted was a thrice-twisted twist.

Now if one of the twists that he twisted *un*twisted,

The untwisted twist would untwist the whole twist."

❧

November 25

Accounting that God was able to raise him up,
even from the dead.
Heb. 11:19

For God so loved the world that He gave His only begotten
Son, that whosoever believeth in Him should not perish,
but have everlasting life.
John 3:16

Is there someone who is dead to the call of God and to all you have tried to do for him or her? Is there something in your own heart that seems dead — hope, faith, courage, gladness, patience, love? These words meet that condition. God is able to raise up even these from the dead.

Think of the infinite love of God. *God so loved the world* — not the good and lovable, but all the people in the world, just as they are. God loves that ungrateful patient, that difficult child, that car driver who doesn't care, that careless workman. God loves those who have disappointed you again and again. Most wonderful of all, God loves you and me.

There are many sorrowful people in the world today, some who have lost their dearest on earth, or who have parted from them. Everywhere there is anxiety. But the power of Calvary suffices for all needs as well as for all sins.

O Love eternal, Love divine,
In wounded hearts pour oil and wine.
Where darkness broods like moonless night,

O Light of Life, let there be light.
And Thine the praise, the glory be
When Thy beloved come home to Thee.

November 26

And they followed vanity, and became vain.
2 Kings 17:15

We will be that which we follow. It does not matter where we are, or what work we are doing. What we follow, that we will become. Follow what is worthless, and we become worthless. Follow truth, love, righteousness, faithfulness, and we will become true, loving, right-living and faithful. Each one of us has a choice.

Choose you this day (Josh. 24:15), for every day we live we become more and more like that which we choose to follow.

November 27

Now, behold, thou trustest upon the staff of this bruised reed,
even upon Egypt, on which if a man lean, it will go into his
hand, and pierce it: so is Pharaoh king of Egypt
unto all that trust on him.
2 Kings 18:21

Rabshakeh, that very horrid man, must have had a
horrid experience. He must have leaned on a reed, and
the reeds that grew along the banks of the Euphrates
were like small bamboos. The reed broke, and the point
ran into the palm of his hand. He would not forget that
stab of pain.

If one leans on anyone, trusting him to stand
strong, and then is disappointed, it is exactly as if a
sharp point had run into one's hand — or heart. It is
a dreadful feeling. *When they took hold of thee . . . thou*
didst break (Ezek. 29:7). That is true of everyone who is
like Rabshakeh's stick.

Do we want to be those whom our Lord can trust
with really difficult things? Those He can depend on not
to break? Then we must practice steadfastness in little
things — in everything. If we do that, we will never be
one of Rabshakeh's sticks.

❧

November 28

For if by one man's offence death reigned by one; much more they which receive abundance of grace and of the gift of righteousness shall reign in life by One, Jesus Christ.
Rom. 5:17

These words were written to ordinary people, many of whom were slaves. Think of a slave's work. Household slaves had to cook great, wasteful feasts and wash up endless dishes. Others had to teach, or to toil hard under an overseer's whip in fields and quarries and on roads. It was hard, lonely, loveless work, and yet Paul told them that they could reign in life.

Every time we conquer a temptation to be lazy, to grumble, to be downhearted, to pity ourselves, to quarrel, to resent being told our faults (which is pure pride), to be ungrateful, to be unfaithful in small things, we *reign in life.* Let us ask for His help through whom alone we can reign in life today.

❧

November 29

*Brethren, I count not myself to have apprehended: but this
one thing I do, forgetting those things which are behind, and
reaching forth unto those things which are before,
I press toward the mark for the prize of the
high calling of God in Christ Jesus.
Phil. 3:13–14*

The old word is true: "For one look at self, take ten
looks at Christ." And yet it is good to let a word like this
of St. Paul's search us.

A true story I read in a book searched me, just as
this word does. A lyrebird made friends with a lady living near Melbourne, Australia, and he used to sing to
her daily. To his own sweet call he added many songs
and calls of other birds. It was a joy to hear him.

In the molting season he went away and his friend
feared that she would never see him again, but to her
delight he returned more wonderful in song than ever.
He had used that time (the most difficult time in a bird's
life) to learn new songs. He had been pressing on.

We too have our molting seasons. How have we
used them? Are we pressing on?

November 30

And he shall be like a tree planted by the rivers of water, that bringeth forth his fruit in his season; his leaf also shall not wither; and whatsoever he doeth shall prosper.
Ps. 1:3

Planted, Kay says, is "properly used of a *transplant-ed* tree." In one sense we are all transplanted. If we are true Christians we have been taken out of the kingdom of darkness and planted in the kingdom of light. But some of us are transplanted in another way. Some are not where they hoped to be, or doing the work they hoped to do. They are tempted to droop, just as a trans-planted tree does when its leaves hang limp. Many are refugees, transplanted in strange lands.

Thank God, He plants His transplanted trees by the River. Kay tells us that the word *rivers* in verse 3 means "branch-canals drawn from a river for irrigation. What river but 'the river of the water of life' — the Spir-it of God? Rev. 22:1." Each transplanted tree has its own irrigation channel, just as in Indian gardens.

When we pray, it is as if we opened the channel a little wider, and perhaps pushed away something that was closing it up. So fresh water can flow to the roots of the transplanted tree, and then its leaves do not droop any more. *His leaf also shall not wither.*

December 1

Be patient therefore, brethren, until the coming of the Lord. Behold, the husbandman waiteth for the precious fruit of the earth, being patient over it, until it receive the early and latter rain.
Jas. 5:7 (RV)

*B*eing patient over it — there is something very loving in these words. Even in Christian circles weakness is often called love, but this kind of love isn't weak. It is the love of the father in the parable of Luke 15. There was no softness in his love, no weakness. He did not reinstate his son till he had utterly forsaken his pride and was broken down by a sense of his sin and unworthiness. But the father's love was *patient over* his prodigal son, never giving up hope.

Our love must be the same.

December 2

*Thy word have I hid in mine heart, that I
might not sin against Thee.*
Ps. 119:11

I rejoice at Thy word, as one that findeth great spoil.
Ps. 119:162

There are many books that we enjoy reading. But none of them can for certain meet us where we are and give us what we need. Never let good books take the place of the Bible. Don't turn to them first in hard hours. Drink from the Well, not from the streams that flow from the Well.

Read thoughtfully, read prayerfully, and soon the Spirit of God will illuminate some verse or passage and you will find in it exactly what you most need.

Take time over your reading. It is deadly to run from text to text, so to speak, without letting the power of the words of our God do their mighty work within us.

Thank God for our Bibles. *Thy word hath quickened me* (Ps. 119: 50).

December 3

And I turned to see the voice that spake with me. And being turned, I saw seven golden candlesticks; and in the midst of the seven candlesticks One like unto the Son of man....And when I saw Him, I fell at His feet as dead. And He laid His right hand upon me, saying unto me, Fear not.... The seven candlesticks which thou sawest are the seven churches.
Rev. 1:12–13, 17, 20

Although the book of Revelation is difficult to understand, it has a wonderful spiritual power to meet us just where we are. The first place where I found this true today was in the first chapter.

We read that John turned to see the Voice which spoke to him, and saw seven golden candlesticks. The golden candlesticks are seven churches: in other words, souls for whom Christ died. Our Lord speaks with us, we turn to see the Voice — and see someone alongside who is needing help. It is John 21:16 in a picture. *Lovest thou Me?...Feed My sheep,* My lambs.

Then as fears came, He whose right hand held the seven stars laid that same hand on His servant, and said, *Fear not.*

Sometimes what we need most is a new sense of the preciousness of His children, for whom our Lord Jesus was content to be betrayed, and given up into the hands of wicked men, and to suffer death upon the cross. There are other times when what we need most is the touch of His wounded hand upon us, and His word, *Fear not.* He knows which is our need today, and He meets our need — He and no other.

December 4

But I trusted in Thee, O Lord: I said, Thou art my God. My times are in Thy hand: deliver me from the hand of mine enemies, and from them that persecute me. Make Thy face to shine upon Thy servant: save me for Thy mercies' sake.
Ps. 31:14–16

It is good to be reminded that our times are in His hand — all the things that are packed into what we call our time. Whether we are old or young, ill or well; whether we are doing the desired or the undesired, the expected or the unexpected — our times are in His hand today and every day.

The Lord *has* delivered us from the hand of our enemies. We are His sheep, and He has said, *My sheep hear My voice, and I know them, and they follow Me: and I give unto them eternal life; and they shall never perish, neither shall any man pluck them out of My hand. My Father, which gave them Me, is greater than all; and no man is able to pluck them out of My Father's hand* (John 10:27–29).

So not only our times, but we ourselves, are safe in His hands today.

December 5

Beloved, let us love one another: for love is of God; and everyone that loveth is born of God, and knoweth God.
1 John 4:7

We all truly seek to live the life of love. But sometimes we can go on fairly comfortably with a sort of spiritual porcupine tucked away in a corner of our heart. (If you want to know what a spiritual porcupine is, look up Psalm 15:3. The psalmist calls it a "Reproach.")

We would not like to keep a pet porcupine, with all its prickles out, under our arm next to our bare skin. But that would be better than going on day after day, giving a still more prickly thing room in our hearts. If we discover that we have a pet porcupine, let us drop it today, and never pick it up again. Love never takes up a Reproach. Love couldn't do that. Love always believes the best. *Beloved, let us love.*

December 6

*He giveth power to the faint; and to them that have no
might He increaseth strength. Even the youths shall faint
and be weary and the young men shall utterly fall: but they
that wait upon the Lord shall renew their strength; they shall
mount up with wings as eagles; they shall run, and not be
weary; and they shall walk, and not faint.*
Isa. 40:29–31

A good deal happened last week which caused some
stress and strain, and I felt rather at the end of everything. I turned to my Bible, and happened to open on
Acts 16:29, *Then he called for a light,* which was exactly
what I was doing.

*Thy word is a lamp unto my feet, and a light unto my
path* (Ps. 119:105). What would be the word of light?
It was a word so familiar that we could all say it back-
wards. But take it for yourself today, and you will find it
as welcome as the lamp which somebody brought that
night to the jailer in the prison of Philippi. It was Isaiah
40:29–31.

❧

December 7

And He spake a parable unto them to this end, that men
ought always to pray, and not to faint.
Luke 18:1

"I don't feel like praying."

Feelings don't matter.

"But I can't pray when I don't feel like it."

Yes, you can. You can say to your Lord, "Lord Jesus, I don't feel like speaking to You. I'm sorry about that. Why is it so?"

"Will He tell me why it is so, if I ask Him?"

Yes, if you really want to know.

"But what about it if I'm not really feeling sorry?"

Never mind your feelings. The one thing that matters is not to stay away from your Lord because of them. Tell Him that your feelings are all wrong and ask Him to put you right. Then stop thinking of yourself and ask Him to bless others, not because of your feelings, but because of His great and wonderful love.

December 8

I will run the way of Thy commandments:
when Thou hast set my heart at liberty.
Ps. 119:32 (BCP)

Even an innocent desire has power to hold our heart in bonds so that we cannot run in spirit. Only our Lord can set our heart at liberty. He can and He does.

Is our spirit in danger of dragging along drearily instead of running gladly to do His bidding? Are we in bondage because of a desire for something which is not His will for us? Turn that word in Psalm 119:32 into a prayer. "O Lord, my Strength and my Redeemer, set my heart at liberty that I may run in the way of Thy commandments."

Now shalt thou see what I will do, will be His word to our hearts then. And we will run, we will sing as we run, for He will put a new song in our mouths, even praise.

December 9

I would have you wise unto that which is good,
and simple concerning evil.
Rom. 16:19

We have to know much that concerns evil. The Bible, all books of history, and the lives of many men called "great" on earth contain things that concern evil, such as the misuse of power, and cruelty, and deceit. The newspapers and the radio also bring us things that are full of grief and evil. How then are we to be as Paul wanted the Roman Christians to be? They too lived in the midst of evil and could not be blind and deaf to it.

Philippians 4:8 answers that question: *Finally, brethren, whatsoever things are true, whatsoever things are honest, whatsoever things are just, whatsoever things are pure, whatsoever things are lovely, whatsoever things are of good report; if there be any virtue, and if there be any praise, think on these things.*

When we hear and read of evil we must sift out the good from the bad and turn our thoughts to the good; then our thought-life will be pleasing to our Lord.

It is impossible to be without knowledge of evil, for *the whole world lieth in wickedness* (1 John 5:19), and we are in the world. But we can shut the door of our thoughts against vile things and think of good things. We can use every reminder of the wickedness of the world as a call to prayer.

December 10

*And sure am I, that, on those who love God, all things are
with one purpose working to bring blessings — yes, on those
to whom, according to His providential plan,
He has cried "Come ye to Me!"*
Rom. 8:28 (Way)

*Why, all things are yours . . . the world, life, death, the im-
mediate present, the far future — all are your heritage: but
you — you belong to no human leader:
you are Messiah's, and Messiah is God's.*
1 Cor. 3:22–23 (Way)

Conybeare's note on those verses in 1 Corinthians
is: "All things work together for the good of Christians;
all things conspire to do them service: but their work is
to do Christ's service, even as He Himself came to do
the will of His Father."

There isn't any exception to that "all." Perhaps today we shall have big things on which to practice faith
in this word. Perhaps it will be little things. Often the
little things get under our guard because we forget that
Romans 8:28 includes them. But whether they are great
or small, it will help if we remember that "all" means *all*,
not some. And so this thing, whatever it be, or however
impossible it seems that it can work for good, is truly
one of the *all things* which conspire to do us service and
bring us blessings.

December 11

But take diligent heed to do the commandment and the law,
which Moses the servant of the Lord charged you, to love the
Lord your God, and to walk in all His ways, and to keep
His commandments, and to cleave unto Him, and to serve
Him with all your heart and with all your soul.
Josh. 22:5

There are some verses which are like boxes of jewels.
Sometimes the jewels are promises, sometimes assurances, sometimes commands. Joshua 22:5 is such a verse. It
shows us in a single sentence the five things which are
required of us, if indeed we are true Christians.

1. To *love* the Lord your God.
2. To *walk* in all His ways.
3. To *keep* His commandments.
4. To *cleave* unto Him.
5. To *serve* Him with all our heart and with all our
   soul.

Five great words: Love, Walk, Keep, Cleave, Serve.
Let us *live* them today.

December 12

Then beware lest thou forget the Lord, which brought thee forth out of the land of Egypt, from the house of bondage.
Deut. 6:12

Let us pay attention to those words, *Then beware.* Like the Israelites in the previous verse, we too are living in houses full of good things which we did not build and fill. We have water without digging wells, and fruit trees which we did not plant. We eat and are full.

Then beware lest thou forget the Lord. He brought us forth out of the land of darkness and the shadow of death, the house of bondage indeed. Let us not forget Him who gave us all that we have: home, flowers, birds, gardens, food, clothes, books, pictures, care when we are ill, joys of all sorts, work to do and strength to do it. A remembering heart is a grateful heart. *Beware lest thou forget.*

December 13

Now Hannah, she spake in her heart; only her lips moved,
but her voice was not heard.
1 Sam. 1:13

Hannah spoke in her heart; only her lips moved. Did you ever wonder why such a tiny thing was told us? Perhaps it was because Satan likes it better when we do just the opposite. He tries to make us content to move our lips without truly speaking in our hearts. That is what he tries to do at all prayer meetings, and singing times, as well as when we pray alone. Don't we sometimes find ourselves singing something just because we like the music? Or joining in a prayer because we know it off by heart?

If so, Hannah has a word for us.

December 14

And Eli said unto her, How long wilt thou be drunken? Put
away thy wine from thee. And Hannah answered and said,
No, my lord, I am a woman of a sorrowful spirit: I have
drunk neither wine nor strong drink, but have poured out
my soul before the Lord. Then Eli answered and said, Go in
peace: and the God of Israel grant thee thy petition that thou
hast asked of Him.... So the woman went her way,
and did eat, and her countenance was no more sad.
1 Sam. 1:14–15, 17–18

Eli misunderstood Hannah, but she was not offended. There isn't anything huffy in her reply. Haven't
we sometimes been quite unlike Hannah in this? Perhaps there wasn't a misunderstanding at all and yet we
took offence. Perhaps there was, and we were angry.
Hannah sets a splendid example to us all. Never take
offence. Always believe the best.

After Hannah had prayed, her countenance was
no longer sad. That is what always should be — but is
it? Do we not sometimes wait to see the answer to our
prayer before letting go of the trouble? Hannah didn't
do that. Long before she saw the answer to her prayer,
she so completely let go of the trouble that there wasn't
a trace of it in her face.

❧

December 15

*And Hannah prayed and said, My heart rejoiceth in
the Lord, mine horn is exalted in the Lord: my mouth is
enlarged over mine enemies; because I rejoice
in thy salvation.*
1 Sam. 2:1

Hannah said this immediately after she had lent Samuel, the son for whom she had prayed, to the Lord for the whole of his life.

Do we always sing when we give up something we love?

It isn't an easy thing to do. Hannah did it, and Hannah rejoiced and said, *My heart rejoiceth in the Lord.*

Bible stories are meant to do something vital for us. Don't let them just float over your mind without doing anything. Say, and mean and do it: "I won't just move my lips in a song or in a prayer: God make me true, like Hannah. I won't take offence when someone says something to me which I don't like; God make me humble-hearted, like Hannah. And when Thou dost ask me to give up something to Thee, by Thy grace I will sing and rejoice, like Hannah."

December 16

But Samuel ministered before the Lord, being a child,
girded with a linen ephod.
1 Sam. 2:18

We are not told everything which that small boy, Samuel, did. We know he opened the doors of the house of the Lord, and in the story in 1 Samuel 3 we are told something that shows his character. He was obedient. When he thought Eli had called him he went to him at once (though I expect he was feeling sleepy), and he said, *Here am I.* That meant: "I'm here. I'm ready to do anything you want me to do."

Samuel was good-tempered even when he was sleepy and had to get up from his bed three times. How do we know that he was good-tempered? Well, after he had come to him three times Eli knew that the Lord had called the child, so he told him what to say if He called him again. And the Lord did call again and He spoke to Samuel and gave him a message to give to Eli. Does the Lord give messages to cross people? I don't think so. So we can be sure that Samuel was good-tempered as well as obedient.

He must have been a humble-minded boy, or he would never have been trusted with such a message to a grown-up person; and he must have been very brave, for he gave the message though he feared. (To be brave doesn't mean that we don't fear, but that we conquer fear.)

Just one thing more: he was truthful, he hid nothing. Obedient, good-tempered, humble, brave, truthful — God make us like Samuel today.

❧

December 17

*And the children of Israel said to Samuel, Cease not to cry
unto the Lord our God for us, that He will save us
out of the hand of the Philistines.*
1 Sam. 7:8

Samuel could not have ceased praying for the children of Israel, even if they had not asked him to pray. He loved the people. We, too, cannot cease to pray for those we love. Our hearts will not let us forget them. This compulsion is of God.

Cease not to cry. The inward urging comes. Yield to it. *Cease not to cry unto the Lord our God.*

Later Samuel said to them, *Moreover as for me, God forbid that I should sin against the Lord in ceasing to pray for you* (1 Sam. 12:23). Samuel never ceased; neither must we.

December 18

*Then all the elders of Israel gathered themselves together, and
came to Samuel unto Ramah, and said unto him, Behold,
thou art old, and thy sons walk not in thy ways: now make
us a king to judge us like all the nations.*
1 Sam. 8:4–5

There was nothing wrong in the other nations having a king, but that was not God's way for the Israelites.
It is pleasant to be *"like all the nations."* It is easier to
float along with the current than to swim up-stream.
But we are not meant to be dead fish, which always do
that. We are meant to be alive and strong enough to do
something very different.

So the first thing is to find out what our God's
thought for us is. Then we must pray and live and work in
accordance with that thought. If we don't, and if instead
we pray for and receive something different, we shall be
like those of whom it is written in Psalm 106:15: *He gave
them their request; but sent leanness into their soul.* How
dreadful it would be to have that sent into our souls.

Why are we here?

To please our Lord in everything.

To lead as many as we can to Him.

To prove by our peaceful life together that it is possible truly to be one in Him.

To prepare to be a company of people who will be
ready to welcome our Lord, and serve during the Thousand Years — and afterwards.

December 19

Teach me to do the thing that pleaseth Thee, for Thou art my
God: let Thy loving Spirit lead me forth
into the land of righteousness.
Ps. 143:10 (BCP)

If we are to please our Lord in everything we must put Him first in everything. There must be an honest acceptance of whatever this means. It means a life with no private reserves, no self-choices — not one. If we are to win souls we must be prepared for what it costs to win them. It cost our Lord Jesus Calvary. It will cost us as much as we are able to bear of what the cross means in daily life. The cross means a daily dying to self and all the claims of self.

Read what our Lord said in Luke 9:23: *If any man will come after Me, let him deny himself* (refuse the voice that urges yielding to anything less than His supreme call to offer all), *and take up his cross daily* (not in one great act of renunciation, but in a thousand unseen and perhaps very small daily acts), *and follow Me.*

Isn't it a comfort to be able to rely on the daily leading of His loving Spirit?

December 20

*If there be therefore any consolation in Christ, if any comfort
of love, if any fellowship of the Spirit, if any bowels and
mercies, fulfill ye my joy, that ye be likeminded, having the
same love, being of one accord, of one mind. Let nothing be
done through strife or vainglory; but in lowliness of mind let
each esteem other better than themselves. Look not every man
on his own things, but every man also on the things of others.
Let this mind be in you, which was also in Christ Jesus.*
Phil. 2:1–5

If we are to prove that it is possible for people from
different parts of the family of God, as well as from
different countries, to live together in happiness, then
what Paul calls the mind of Christ must be in us.

"Mind" there means "forbearance, gentleness, yield-
ingness." This does not mean that we are to be jellyfish,
things without backbone, flabby. It does not mean that
convictions are to be watered down till they disappear.
But it does mean that in each of us there must be a gentleness, an inner sweetness that cannot possibly harbor
an unkind thought, and a brave and generous love like
our Lord's.

The next verses, Philippians 2:6-8, show us His
love. That is our pattern. *Let this mind be in you, which
was also in Christ Jesus.*

December 21

*And why call ye Me, Lord, Lord, and
do not the things which I say?*
Luke 6:46

There are many things which our Lord said; let us
look out for them as we read the Gospels. One of the
things He said comes earlier in the same chapter (Luke
6:31): *And as ye would that men should do to you, do ye
also to them likewise.*

If we do not obey this word, instantly troubles crop
up, little roots of bitterness that will soon grow large
and strong. Sometimes we disobey in thought only, and
so we think it does not matter. But it does. What we
think colors what we *say* and *do*, because, after all, what
we think is what we *are*.

There is one question that is easy to answer. Would
you like others to think kindly of you, or unkindly?
Hardly or tenderly? Then, as you would that others
should do to you, do you also to them likewise. *This* is
to do one of the most important things which our Lord
says to each one of us.

December 22

*Of the sons of Asaph, the singers were over the business
of the house of God.*
Neh. 11:22

I will sing a new song unto Thee, O God.
Ps. 144:9

*Speaking to yourselves in psalms and hymns and spiritual
songs, singing and making melody in your heart to the Lord.*
Eph. 5:19

Singing with grace in your hearts to the Lord.
Col. 3:16

Singing people do practical work. The singers were
over the business of the house of God. You who are being busy all day long about common things for love of
Him, isn't it good to know that you are singers and He
is listening to your song? Your new song? I will sing
unto the Lord a new song.

There is always something new to sing about. God's
singers are the happiest people in all the world. Even
when they can't sing so that others hear, it doesn't matter. *Singing and making melody in your heart to the Lord*
makes that clear.

The Lord give us grace in our hearts so that we may
be His singers today.

December 23

Now therefore fear ye not: I will nourish you, and your little
ones. And he [Joseph] comforted them,
and spake kindly unto them.
Gen. 50:21

I will nourish you, and your little ones, said the earthly Joseph to his troubled brothers, and he comforted them and spoke kindly to them. How often, how very often, has our heavenly Joseph, who is not ashamed to call us brethren (Heb. 2:11), said these words to us. Year by year He has nourished us and our little ones. We have lacked nothing.

Pain stands behind this lavish love. Calvary stands behind it. Joseph foreshadows a greater Sufferer. *The archers have sorely grieved him, and shot at him, and hated him* (Gen. 49:23).

This Christmas month, when we shall so fully and joyfully see the loving nourishing of us and our little ones, let us remember Calvary and live in spirit and in truth in the dust at the foot of the cross.

December 24

*Jesus saith unto them, My meat is to do the will of Him
that sent Me, and to finish His work.*
John 4:34

*For I came down from heaven, not to do Mine own will,
but the will of Him that sent Me.*
John 6:38

The words are for all of us. *My meat,* my very food,
the thing I cannot do without, *is to do the will of Him
that sent me, and to finish His work* — not to leave it half
done. It is so easy to do nothing because one cannot do
much — and that also is not to finish His work.

To do His work requires a definite and repeated
turning away from our own will. "I came down from
heaven, *not to do Mine own will,* but the will of Him
that sent Me." It will mean a daily choice, perhaps an
hourly choice, of something which is not our own will
at all. It will mean faithfulness, patience, courage. The
Lord give us hour by hour these great virtues.

⤬

December 25

For Christmas Day

Did Mary say to Joseph tenderly,
"Such little hands, such little feet! They be
Like little shells we've found beside the sea,
The sea of Galilee"?

And did wise Joseph answer, "For love's sake
   Our love shall shelter Him, enclose, and hold,
As the low hills about that silver lake
   Shelter it, fold on fold"?

      Across the stable, like a wind — a breath —
      "The wicked have enclosed Me," it saith.
      "Thou hast brought Me into the dust of death."
         Into the dust of death.

And then did Joseph's father-like surprise,
   As round his finger little fingers curled,
Call smiles and tears to Mary's mother-eyes?
   He clings who'll save the world.

And as the Child in His soft manger lay,
Did gentle oxen in their language say,
"A mangerful of our sweet-smelling hay —
 Our gift this Christmas Day"?

      Again that breath — An unregarded tree
      Is growing somewhere, making wood to be,
      One awful day, the cross of Calvary.
         The cross of Calvary.

O Lord, we adore Thee!
The wicked did enclose Thee;
Pierced were Thy hands and feet for us — for me —
O Child of Bethlehem,
Christ our dear Redeemer,
We come and we adore Thee,
We come and we adore Thee,
We come and we adore Thee,
   Christ our Lord.

December 26

Finally, my brethren, let your hearts be strengthened in the Lord, and in the conquering power of His might.
Eph. 6:10 (Conybeare)

Let not your heart be troubled.
John 14:1

Sometimes we do not feel strong, and we do feel troubled. Conybeare says the literal meaning of the Greek words in Ephesians 6:10 is *Let your hearts be strengthened in the Lord.* That reminds us of our Lord's own words; and His commands are His enablings. So let us obey His word today, however weak we feel.

Let not your heart be troubled.

Let your hearts be strengthened in the Lord, and in the conquering power of His might. Alleluia!

December 27

For God gave us not a spirit of cowardice, but a spirit of power and love and self-restraint.
2 Tim. 1:7 (Conybeare)

"*Self-restraint* would control the passion of *fear*" is Conybeare's note. What is the spirit of cowardice? Surely it is the spirit that looks into the future asking, "But what will happen if...?"

God save us from the spirit of cowardice. It should be harder for us to doubt His power and love than to believe in His grace and might. The God who has done so much for us, He will be in our future as He has been in our past. Let us count on the Lord our God, and gladly receive from Him His Spirit of power and love and self-restraint which conquers fear.

December 28

For He maketh sore, and bindeth up: He woundeth,
and His hands make whole.
Job 5:18

The book of Job is full of words which God Himself says are not right (Job 42:7), and one has to be
continually disentangling truth from falsehood. None
of Job's friends distinguished between God's will and
God's permission — that is, what He did not plan, but
allowed to happen for His greater glory and Job's greater
good and the help of countless millions. Sometimes in
a single sentence they mixed up things right and wrong,
and their beautiful words have to be used with care lest
they be not as true as they are beautiful.

Poor Job, how weary he grew of them! Have you
ever thanked God that when you are ill or in trouble
you have real friends about you, and never have to sit on
an ash pit and be told how bad you are?

A good example of the mix-up is in the sentence,
He woundeth, and His hands make whole. This is often
given to sick people to comfort them, but there is no
comfort in it. If the wound is His doing, then what
right have we to take anything to ease it? Eliphaz took
it for granted that God's hand had wounded Job, but
as we know from chapter 1:12, it wasn't God's hand. It
was Satan's, though God allowed it in order to fulfill His
own great purposes.

The second half of Eliphaz's remark was perfectly true. The hand of our God does make whole. His is the skill that guides the hands of doctors and nurses. His is the wisdom that discovers the healing properties of plants and other things He has put in the world. All the wounding is His enemy's. All the healing is His.

❧

December 29

Behold, I go forward, but He is not there; and backward, but I cannot perceive Him: on the left hand, where He doth work, but I cannot behold Him; He hideth Himself on the right hand, that I cannot see Him; but He knoweth the way that I take: when He hath tried me, I shall come forth as gold.
Job 23:8–10

Eliphaz had heaped up words twice already and Job must have been very weary of him. Yet in chapter 22:21–30 he speaks most beautifully. People often quote those words, which lose their beauty when we remember their unfairness. Eliphaz takes it for granted that Job has left God and therefore is suffering, and will continue to suffer till he returns to Him. But how can one return who hasn't gone away? Job's greatest griefs came when he was very near his God. His children were feasting, and at such times it was his custom to rise up early to pray for them. *Thus did Job continually* (ch. 1:5).

So all through Eliphaz's beautiful talk runs a thread of untruth. He did not speak the thing that was right. He wounded Job by his cruel misunderstanding of the whole perplexing set of circumstances.

It is good to see how Job turns from the misunderstanding of man to the perfect understanding of God. He cannot see Him or find Him, *but* — glorious "but" — *He knoweth the way that I take.* And in the end Job did come forth as gold.

December 30

But I would ye should understand, brethren, that the things
which happened unto me have fallen out rather to the
furtherance of the gospel; so that my bonds in Christ are
manifest in all the palace, and in all other places.
Phil. 1:12–13

Job's fourth friend, Elihu, is the least objectionable.
His thoughts of God are higher than those of the other
three, and so, apparently, he did not need to have a sacrifice offered on his behalf. But he misunderstood Job's
sufferings just as the other three did. He inferred that
God caused it. But God sums him up thus: *Who is this*
that darkeneth counsel by words without knowledge? (Job
38:2).

The puzzle is, why is the enemy given the power to
hurt God's children? Poor Job had no light on that, but
Paul, in Nero's prison, had confidence that what seemed
so hindering was really helping the people he loved so
much.

It needs faith to take this stand with Paul about
our own much lighter trials, and the trials of those we
love. But though we may not in the least understand,
we can believe. The more steadfastly we believe, against
all appearances and feelings, the more we find *all joy and*
peace in believing (Rom. 15:13).

❦

December 31

*Wherefore we receiving a kingdom which cannot be moved,
let us have grace, whereby we may serve God acceptably
with reverence and godly fear.*
Heb. 12:28

"Serve God well pleasingly" is Young's Literal Translation. How can such work as I can do be ever even a little pleasing, much less *well* pleasing, to the holy Father? As we look back through the year and see only and always such poor service, unpleasing even to us, our one comfort is in His forgiveness.

As so often, our little children can help us. We all know what kind of ducks and cows and elephants and giraffes they draw, and what extraordinary people, and what curious flowers. Sometimes we cannot recognize them at all unless they write underneath *duck, cows,* and so on. And yet when they bring them to us we are pleased — well pleased. We see their love, their eagerness, their wish to please us. Perhaps it is like this with our Heavenly Father, only of course we must not be content to continue indefinitely as nursery school children.

As we enter this New Year let us make Hebrews 13:20–21 our prayer: *Now the God of Peace...make you perfect in every good work to do His will, working in you that which is well-pleasing in His sight, through Jesus Christ; to whom be glory for ever and ever. Amen.*

Index of Biblical References

Index

Index

Index

Index

Index

Index

Index

This book was produced by CLC Publications. We hope it has been life-changing and has given you a fresh experience of God through the work of the Holy Spirit. CLC Publications is an outreach of CLC Ministries International, a global literature mission with work in over 50 countries. If you would like to know more about us or are interested in opportunities to serve with a faith mission, we invite you to contact us at:

CLC Ministries International
P.O. Box 1449
Fort Washington, PA 19034

Phone: (215) 542-1242
E-mail: orders@clcpublications.com
Website: www.clcpublications.com

- - - - - - - - - - - - - - - - - - - -

DO YOU LOVE GOOD CHRISTIAN BOOKS?
Do you have a heart for worldwide missions?

You can receive a FREE subscription to
CLC's newsletter on global literature missions
Order by e-mail at:

clcworld@clcusa.org

Or fill in the coupon below and mail to:

P.O. Box 1449
Fort Washington, PA 19034

FREE *CLCWORLD* SUBSCRIPTION!

Name: _____

Address:_____

_____

Phone: _____ Email:_____

READ THE REMARKABLE STORY OF

the founding of

CLC International

"Any who doubt that Elijah's God still lives ought to read of the money supplied when needed, the stores and houses provided, and the appearance of personnel in answer to prayer."—Moody Monthly

Is it possible that the printing press, the editor's desk, the Christian bookstore and the mail order department can glow with the fast-moving drama of an "Acts of the Apostles"?

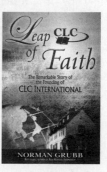

Find the answer as you are carried from two people in an upstairs bookroom to a worldwide chain of Christian bookcenters multiplied by nothing but a "shoestring" of faith and by committed, though unlikely, lives.

The Dohnavur Fellowship

The work in Dohnavur still continues, but now the Fellowship members are all of Indian nationality. They do not belong officially to any of the organized churches; but in fellowship with others of God's children, they seek to make His love and salvation known to all whom they can reach.

The dedication of girls to the temples is now illegal, but the Fellowship provides a home for children who might otherwise fall into the hands of people who would exploit them in some way.

Girls of all ages from babies to teenagers form a large part of the family in Dohnavur. The need to care for them continues until they are securely launched elsewhere or else have become fellow workers. The aim is still to bring them up to know and love our Lord Jesus and to follow His example as those who desire not to be served but to serve others.

The hospital treats patients from the surrounding countryside. They are from varied religious backgrounds—Hindu, Muslim, Christian. They include rich and poor, highly educated and illiterate. Through this medical work God continues to bring to us the people we long to reach, those whose need is for spiritual as well as physical healing.

Boys are no longer admitted, but the buildings they occupied are now put to full use. In 1981 the Fellowship in partnership with other Christians formed the Santhosha Educational Society to administer a coeducational English-medium boarding school, primarily for the benefit of the children of missionaries of Indian nationality. The buildings provide facilities for over 600 children now studying there. Their parents come from Indian missions and organizations working in many parts of India, including tribal areas.

In matters of finance, we follow the pattern shown from the beginning of the work. Amy Carmichael rejoiced in her Heavenly Father's faithfulness in supplying each need. We praise Him that His faithfulness is the same today.

The Dohnavur Fellowship
Tirunelveli District
Tamil Nadu 627 102
India

The Dohnavur Fellowship
80 Windmill Road
Brentford, Middlesex
TW8 0QH
England

http://www.dohnavurfellowship.org

Books by Amy Carmichael